ISAIAH
Wolfgang Roth

KNOX PREACHING GUIDES
John H. Hayes, Editor

John Knox Press
ATLANTA

Unless otherwise indicated Scripture quotations are translations from the Hebrew by the author.

Library of Congress Cataloging-in-Publication Data

Roth, Wolfgang. 1930–
   Isaiah / Wolfgang Roth.
     p. cm.—(Knox preaching guides)
   Bibliography: p.
   ISBN 0-8042-3221-0
   1. Bible. O.T. Isaiah—Homiletical use. 2. Bible. O.T. Isaiah—Commentaries. I. Title. II. Series.
BS1515.5.R67   1988
224′.107—dc19   87-28093
                                                                             CIP

© copyright John Knox Press 1988
10 9 8 7 6 5 4 3 2 1
Printed in the United States of America
John Knox Press
Atlanta, Georgia 30365

Contents

Introduction	1
The Book of Isaiah in Church and Synagogue	1
A Vision of the Whole: The Composition	3
Isaiah 1—66 and "The Law and the Prophets"	5
Thematic Structure	7
The Use of Guide- and Framewords	9
"First and Second Isaiah"—Discourse and Source Analysis	11
The Center and the Circle: A Theology of Isaiah 1—66	12
The Audience	12
The Speaker	13
The Argumentation	16
The Vision of the Lord's Vineyard	18
Preaching from Isaiah 1—66	19
The Use of the Guide	20
Recommended Translations	21
Sermon Suggestions	21
The Title of the Book: The Vision of Isaiah (1:1)	25
Prologue: The Future of the Deserted City (1:2–4:6)	28
The Exaltation of Apostate Zion (1:2—2:5)	28
The Miracle of a Remnant (1:2–9)	28
The Peril of Selective Obedience (1:10–20)	29
The Certainty of Refinement (1:21–31)	30
The Future of Zion's Peace (2:1–4)	31
New Lease on an Ancient Shelter (2:5—4:6)	33
Reversals of Perspective (2:6–22)	33
The Dishonor of Judah's Men (3:1–15)	35
The Disgrace of Zion's Women (3:16–4:1)	36
The Transformation of Mount Zion (4:2–6)	37
Part I: The Vision of Israel's Future and of Its Peaceable Mountain (5:1—27:13)	39
The Deserted Vineyard and the Shoot of Jesse (5:1—12:6)	39
Isaiah's Mandate in the Lord's Vineyard (5:1—9:6)	39

Isaiah's Vision of the Lord's Peace (9:7—12:6)	51
The Invitation to the Chastised Nations (13:1—27:13)	59
The Rout of the Nations (13:1—23:18)	60
The Banquet for All the Nations (24:1—27:13)	79
Part II: The Vision of Assyria's Withdrawal and Jerusalem's Rescue (28:1—37:38)	88
The Lord's Call to Feasting in Zion (28:1—35:10)	88
The Woes over the Lord's Adversaries (28:1—33:9)	89
The Invitation to the City of Assembly (33:10—35:10)	103
Narrative Review of Sennacherib's Humiliation (36:1—37:38)	109
Isaiah 36–37/38–39 as Conceptual Link and Literary Hinge	109
Historical Background	110
The Double Challenge of 36:1—37:38	111
Part III: The Vision of Babylon's Fall and Zion's Restoration (38:1—55:13)	115
Narrative Preview of Judah's Exile to Babylon (38:1—39:8)	115
Hezekiah's Miraculous Recovery (38:1—22)	116
The Announcement of Judah's Future Exile to Babylon (39:1–8)	117
Release into a New Creation (40:1—55:13)	118
The Mission of the Servant (40:1—47:15)	119
The Call of Abraham's Kin (48:1—55:13)	139
Epilogue: The Presence of Zion's Future (56:1—66:24)	157
The Ascent of the Lord's City (56:1—60:22)	157
The Lord's Peace for the Far and the Near (56:1—57:21)	157
The Lord's Acceptance of the Contrite (58:1—59:21)	160
The Invitation to Zion's Radiance (60:1–22)	165
The Center of Worldwide Israel (61:1—66:24)	168
The Announcement of Israel's Liberation (61:1—63:6)	168
Liturgy of a New Creation (63:7–65:25)	172
The Elusive Divine Presence (66:1–24)	177
Bibliography	181

ISAIAH

Introduction

The Book of Isaiah in Church and Synagogue

Next to the Psalter, the Book of Isaiah is among Christians the best known writing of the OT. With its words the advent of Jesus as the Prince of Peace is celebrated, with its portrayal of the suffering of the Lord's servant the passion of Good Friday is described, and with its image of the Peaceable Kingdom the hope for a world healed and restored is given shape (8:23b—9:6; 52:13—53:12; 11:1-9). Little wonder that passages from Isaiah are well represented in lectionaries, that men and women versed in the Scriptures cherish the book, and that preachers of diverse persuasions turn to it for inspiration and study.

The NT writings share this predilection. Phrases or sentences from almost every chapter of Isaiah are either quoted or alluded to in this collection of normative writings of the early Church (see the suggested sermon series on "The Work of Jesus in Isaiah's Words"). Furthermore, motifs prominent in Isa 1—66 have become points of departure for conceptualizations of notable themes in some NT books. Thus the parable chapter in the Gospel of Mark (4:1-34) provides the setting for Jesus' discourse on "the hardening of the heart" (compare Mark 4:10-12 with Isa 6:9-10), and the narration about the Ethiopian eunuch (Acts 8:26-39) portrays that pilgrim to Jerusalem puzzling over the identity of "the suffering servant" about whom he is reading in the Book of Isaiah (compare Acts 8:37 with Isa 53:7–8).

Also, groups within early Judaism read and pondered the book because it affirmed expectations of Israel's future restoration under "anointed ones." One such group was the community which flourished for some two hundred years before 73 C.E. at the northwestern shore of the Dead Sea, and whose library, the Dead Sea Scrolls, provides information concerning their communal life, their Scriptures, and their beliefs. Almost all the books of the Hebrew Bible are represented among the scrolls, usually though as fragments. The Book of Isaiah, however, is preserved in a nearly complete scroll (1QIs^a). And while this find does not in itself prove that members of the community held Isaiah in special esteem, their interests in "anointed ones" (Messiah[s]) who were to come must have given to Isaiah an important place in their reflections.

Preaching on texts from the Book of Isaiah, one is thus heir to a lively tradition of interpretation in both Synagogue and Church. Stories about the prophet and especially his martyrdom were already told in early Jewish and Christian circles. For example, the Jewish-Christian apocryphal work "Martyrdom and Ascension of Isaiah" first tells how the prophet was cut in two with a saw at the order of King Manasseh and then relates how Isaiah, during King Hezekiah's reign, had ascended to the seventh heaven, there seeing the future descent to earth of the Lord (Jesus) and of the Holy Spirit (see *The Old Testament Pseudepigrapha* [ed. by J. H. Charlesworth, 1985] vol. 2, pp. 143–76, for this sample of a free development of Isaiah themes in the service of Jewish and Christian preaching). Other examples are found in Louis Ginzberg's retelling of *The Legends of the Jews* (1913) vol. 4, pp. 270–77, as they relate to Isaiah and his royal contemporary King Hezekiah; they show how encounters between a pious king and a commanding prophet were retold and developed in the service of instruction and exhortation in the first centuries of Synagogue and Church. In these ancient narratives we encounter, as it were, the first preaching guides on Isaiah!

Of the making of commentaries on Isaiah there is no end! We note only well-known Christian theologians whose commentaries have been preserved: Origen (third century C.E.), Jerome (fifth century C.E.), Thomas Aquinas (thirteenth century C.E.), Luther, Zwingli, and Calvin (sixteenth century C.E.). These commentaries, as well as those written since the Reformation, are still instructive and useful today, although they reflect—as almost all commentaries do—the ecclesiastic and dogmatic concerns of their authors.

On the other hand, many commentaries written in the last one hundred years employ literary-historical methods. They seek to trace the genesis of the work from its beginnings in small, oral units to its final redaction as a composition of considerable length, engaging in what may broadly be called "source analysis." This preaching guide differs from earlier commentaries (see the Bibliography for a selection), being based on what may be called "discourse analysis." It is contextual-compositional in approach, making the whole of the book the primary horizon of interpretation, while acknowledging within the work differences of perspective, vocabulary, and style. In other words, this guide is first of all concerned with "a vision of the whole" (Isa 29:11)—a telling phrase found in the work itself. This phrase can serve as a guideword for the following discussion of the composition of Isa 1—66.

A Vision of the Whole: The Composition

As a work of literary art, the book must indeed have been born of a vision! It is no accident that it is introduced by that very term: "The Vision of Isaiah the son of Amoz" (1:1). The vision is attributed to a man named Isaiah son of Amoz, who as a contemporary of Kings Uzziah, Jotham, Ahaz, and Hezekiah was active during the last half of the eighth century B.C.E. The memory of his words and actions was alive through generations among his disciples (see 8:11–23c; 26:7–10; 48:16b; 50:4–9, 59:21). They were the persons in whose reflections and writings the work took shape in its conceptual and literary-compositional unity. That conception is the triply attested assurance that Jerusalem is the center of worldwide Judaism, forever secure as "the city of our assemblies" (33.17). Was not the paradigm of its divine protection evident for the first time in its deliverance from the aggressive Aramean-Ephraimite coalition in 733 B.C.E, then for the second time in its miraculous escape from almost certain conquest by the Assyrian army in 701 B.C.E., and finally for the third time in its restoration in 538/520 B.C.E. under King Cyrus of Persia, "the Lord's anointed one" (45:1)?

What binds Isa 1—66 into a conceptual unity is the conviction that these deliverances are incidents of one and the same paradigm of divine intervention on Zion's behalf. And it is of that conceptual matrix that the literary shape of the work is born. Thus the themes of the three deliverances become the organizing elements of the work's three parts: the first deliverance in 5:1—27:13, the second in 28:1—38:37, and the third in 38:1—56:12. By the same token, the two text units which precede and follow the book's tripartite main body may be identified as prologue (1:2—4:6) and epilogue (56:1—66:24).

The Lord's deliverance of Jerusalem, thus repeatedly attested, is the master theme of Isa 1—66. Can it fail to open blind eyes and darkened minds so that they perceive the Lord God of Israel at work and the invitation to assemble in the Lord's worship on Mount Zion (32:3–5; 35:5–7; 42:18–25; 61:1–3)?

Though a sizeable and sustained writing in its own right, the book presents itself as part of a still larger composition. The word-for-word repetition of almost three chapters of 2 Kings within the book (in 36:1—39:8) alerts readers to the connection between Isa 1—66 and that literary work of which 2 Kings 18—20 is a part. Since the same kind of repetition also connects the Book of Jeremiah to the same larger work (Jer 52:1–34 = 2 Kings 24:18—25:30), the doubling must be explored and related to the interpretation of Isa 1—66.

Furthermore, a comparison of Isa 36—39 with the rest of the book shows that many of its texts are formulated and grouped into units which thematically resemble the sequence of narrative motifs in 36—39. This central section not only links Isa 1—66 to a larger literary work, but also provides an important internal compositional pattern for Isa 1—66.

Thus Isa 36—39 is compositionally important in two different, though related, ways. Far from being insignificant as an appendix to the book, it is the key to both the internal structure of the book and the book's role in its larger context. Both call for elaboration. We turn first to a discussion of the Book of Isaiah as part of a still more comprehensive composition.

Isaiah 1—66 and "The Law and the Prophets"

The large work to which Isa 1—66 belongs is the extended narrative which is preserved in its sequential integrity in the Hebrew Bible—and only there. In the Synagogue (and in the NT) it is known as "The Law and the Prophets." It is made up of these twenty-four (twice twelve) components: Genesis–Exodus–Leviticus–Numbers–Deuteronomy–Joshua–Judges–(1, 2) Samuel–(1, 2) Kings–Isaiah–Jeremiah–Ezekiel–"The Twelve" (Minor Prophets: Hosea–Joel–Amos–Obadiah–Jonah–Micah–Nahum–Habakkuk–Zephaniah–Haggai–Zechariah–Malachi). Since Christian Bibles follow the Greek Scriptures of Hellenistic Judaism (the Septuagint) in presenting some writings in a different order, the work "The Law and the Prophets" does not appear there in the sequential integrity it has in the Hebrew Bible. However, users of Christian Bibles can readily read the work in its sequential integrity by passing over those components which are not in the above list.

Contrary to what the compound title suggests, "The Law and the Prophets" is not a bipartite work but presents itself as one continuous, sustained narration. It moves, as it were, from one pole to another, from creation to re-creation. The narrative proceeds within a (on the whole) consistently constructed framework of narrated time and space, presenting one set of actors and developing a broad, though focused, design. The plot is a winning of a new heaven and a new earth after the first heaven and earth have been squandered. Or, in John Milton's words, "Paradise Lost—Paradise Regained."

The motifs which constitute the overarching design are familiar to Bible readers: creation and disobedience—deluge and dispersion—obedience and blessing (so Gen 1—25, the prologue of the work). Its main body (Genesis 25–Zechariah) is made up of two thematically parallel motif sequences. The first part is Genesis 25–Joshua; its motif sequence may be summarized in this manner: Israel's birth and enslavement—

redemption and covenant—disobedience, punishment, and renewal of covenant. The second part is Judges–Zechariah; it develops a corresponding motif sequence in relation to the rise, existence, and demise of human kingship in Israel and Judah. Malachi is the epilogue of the work.

The title "The Law and the Prophets" is indeed ancient; it is attested in 2 Macc 15:9 (Septuagint/Apocrypha) and Matt 5:17 (NT); compare Megillah 4:1–4 (Mishnah). However, it is post-biblical because it is not found in the Hebrew Bible. Hence the question: does the work contain its (original) title? Since sometimes the name of a work appears in its epilogue (see, for example, Sir 50:27; John 20:30–31), one looks to Malachi for guidance. There it is said in 3:13–21 (RSV: 3:13—4:3) that those who remained loyal to the Lord God of Israel were deeply troubled by the assertion of those who were ready to forsake their inherited faith by claiming that "it is vain to serve God." In response to the despondency of the loyal, "a book of remembrance was written before him for (or of) those who are faithful to the Lord and think on his name." It will enable them "to distinguish between those who are loyal to God and those who are not, between one who serves God and one who does not."

Is "a book of remembrance" the name of the comprehensive composition Genesis–Zechariah which indeed contains all one needs to know in order to make this distinction? Does it not offer illustration after illustration, culled from the memory of exilic Israel, of loyal service as well as of apostasy—beginning with the first created human beings and ending with examples from the immediate past? Moreover, does this summary title of the whole composition not precede the concluding, backward- and forward-looking reference to the Law of Moses and to the expectation of the return of Elijah, the prophet (Mal 3:22–24 [RSV:4:4–6])? At any rate, in keeping with its encyclopedic function of collecting and preserving Israel's memories in times of exile and dispersion, the voluminous composition is theologically and, as far as possible, also literarily, unified. It is, as it were, a first "Encyclopedia Judaica"!

What is the function of Isa 1—66 within "A Book of Remembrance"? The introduction of the book as "The Vision of

Isaiah son of Amoz" (1:1) relates to an important theological issue found in the larger work, that of the legitimation of a prophetic vision as divine revelation. After all, the primary revelation of the Lord's will for Israel is located once for all in the face-to-face encounter between God and Moses, the archprophet (Deut 34:10; compare Num 12:7–8 and Exod 33:7–11). By the same token, the Lord's self-disclosure through other prophets is considered valid only when it is mediated through "a vision" (Num 12:6). In other words, the divine revelation through prophets is both legitimated by and subordinated to the direct self-disclosure granted to Moses.

Thus the position of Isa 1—66 within "A Book of Remembrance"—and at the place where it stands—is a considered placement. It identifies Isa 1—66, the smaller work in comparison to the larger one, as a composition which serves as vindication for a central premise of the "Book of Remembrance." This is also the reason why Isa 1—66 is introduced and classed as "a vision" and why obedience to the law of the Lord is occasionally stressed (1:10; 5:24; 30:9 51:4). In short, the Book of Isaiah presents itself as a duly, that is, scripturally, validated "vision." The vision depicts the holy city's escapes from three successive threats as a result of divine interventions, thus confirming the Lord's protection of Mount Zion.

Thematic Structure

The central passage, 36—39, provides the key for understanding the composition of the entire Book of Isaiah. It consists of two parts: the narrative of the divine deliverance of Zion from the assault of Sennacherib, King of Assyria (36:1—37:38), and the following story, loosely coordinated in narrated time with the one which precedes it, of the Lord's deliverance of the Judaite King Hezekiah from a mortal illness—a story which was to have an ominous aftermath (38:1—39:8).

A sequence of five motifs appears in both parts: (1) extreme threat (36:1–20 [with motif repetition in 37:9b–13] and 38:1), (2) submissive appeal to the Lord through Isaiah (36:21—37:5 [with motif repetition in 37:14–20] and 38:2–3), (3) divine assurance of a favorable intervention, attested by a sign (37:6–8 and 38:4–8a), (4) poetic celebration of the certainty of divine rescue (37:21–35 and 38:9–20), and finally (5) narration of the Lord's intervention (37:36–37 and 38:8b–21). The short story of the Babylonian embassy, its reception by Hezekiah, and Isaiah's condemnation of the king's action concludes with a preview of 40—55, the Babylonian threat to Jerusalem and its royal house. Thus Isaiah's announcement to Hezekiah extends the duration of the divine rescue of Zion and Judah until "the days to come," when exile to Babylonia would become an even more serious threat to the life of city and nation.

While Isa 36—39 is in this manner linked by way of preview to the third part of the book (40—55), it is also connected to its first part (5—27). The link is created through the use of a phrase which stands out: "at/near the conduit of the Upper Pool by the road of the Fullers' Field" (36:2b = 7:3b); its appearance in both the first and the second parts of the book parallels, as it were, the two rescues. Moreover, the three threats to the city are thus serialized into a sequence of increasing severity.

Apart from the forward and backward connections of 36—39, its internal (and doubled) fivefold narrative motif sequence is significant. The movement from (1) threat to (2) castigation, then to (3) supplication, and eventually to (4) intervention and (5) consolation characterizes not only 36—39 but also text units elsewhere in the book. In fact, the alternation of rebuke and comfort, observable throughout the book, gives it the internal thematic rhythm which even casual readers cannot but notice.

The following discussion of several examples of this thematic patterning will substantiate the thesis. In the section Isa 28–35 which presents the Lord's call to festal joy in Zion, six "woe!" units appear in the first part (28:1; 29:1; 29:15; 30:1; 31:1; and 33:1); they are addressed to different groups of people and castigate them in various ways. These reproaches are, however, balanced by increasingly clearer and stronger assurances of divine rescue. The words of comfort are at first formulated in a somewhat veiled fashion (28:23–

29; 29:13–14), then more openly (30:19–33) and fully (31:4—32:20), and finally in exuberance (33:17–24; 35:1–10).

Another example is the section "The Restoration of the Devastated Vineyard" (5—12). Its compositional flow moves from chastisement (such as the parable of the unworthy vineyard; 5:1–7) through the call to submission to a radical threat (such as Isaiah's counsel in the face of the Aramean-Ephraimite siege, 7:1–9) to affirmations of future peace and well-being (for instance, the announcement of the birth of the Prince of Peace [8:23b—9:6] or of David's peaceable kingdom [11-1–16]); it is concluded by songs of celebration which echo the victory songs of the Red Sea (12:1–3).

A final example of a larger section is the prologue of the work where, as is the nature of a preview, characteristic features stand out more clearly. "The Future of the Deserted City" (1:2—4:6) is divided into two parts, largely parallel with each other (1:2—2:5, 2:6—4:6). Both move from summary castigation (1:2–31; 2:6—4:1) to comprehensive assurance (2:1–5; 4:2–6); thus illustrating pointedly the thematic alternation which is typical for all of Isa 1—66.

On the other hand, smaller units also are often constructed according to the pattern "chastisement–promise." For instance, the text 42:18—44:23 opens with a (gentle) reprimand of the Lord's blind and deaf servant (42:18–25), then describes the coming divine intervention in contrast to the idols' impotence (43:1—44:8, 9–20), recalling for the servant the Lord's demonstrated power (44:21–22), and then concludes with a call to celebration of the Lord's intervention (44:23).

In sum, Isa 1—66 is to a large extent in its longer and shorter text units molded by the pattern "From Threat and Castigation to Deliverance and Assurance." That design is laid out narratively in 36—38 and poetically in the prologue (1:2—4:6). The observations made in the preaching guide below, as well as the Table of Contents, reflect this insight.

The Use of Guide- and Framewords

A characteristic feature of biblical literature generally and of Isa 1—66 specifically is the use of guidewords. The repetition of a word or a phrase identifies not only the theme but also the limits of its text unit.

Martin Buber's discussion of this formative element in biblical literary creativity shows how variations of a wordroot can permeate and delineate a text unit, capturing and centering various aspects of that which is told or sung (*Werke*, vol. 2 [1964], 1131–49). An English equivalent would be the repeated use of a word such as "light" or of words containing that semantic element (such as "enlighten," "lights," "lightning," and "lit") in such a manner that the guideword(s) define(s) the unit as well as emphasize(s) its thrust. For example, the passage "The Invitation to Zion's Light" (60:1–22) illustrates through its sevenfold use of the guideword "light" how that notion defines that passage.

Another instance is the fourfold use of "weary" in 40:27–31. Occasionally, a guideword is turned into a pun by changing one of its consonants or reversing the order of two of them, in either case creating words with the opposite meaning, such as "equity/iniquity" in 5:1–7 and "ashes/eminence" in 61:1–3. The best known guideword—or rather guidephrase—which provides a broad, thematic unity to the entire book is "The Holy One of Israel" (see 1:4; 12:6; 30:12; 41:14; 54:4; 60:14).

The doubling of a word is another example of the use of guidewords. This feature occurs especially in the third part (38:1—55:13) and in the epilogue. Thus the opening line of "The Vision of Babylon's Fall" (40:1—55:13) begins with the repeated command, "Comfort ye, comfort ye my people!" From then on examples abound (see, for example, 48:11; 52:11; 57:14; and 62:10; but also 21:9). The heightening effect of this compositional device is also evident in refrain-like repetitions of lines or double lines, combining smaller units into series; see especially the two "woe!" sequences in 5:8–24 and 28:1—33:8, as well as the four (five) refrains in 9:7—10:4 (5:25b). These replications give the book not only an element of stylistic uniqueness but also a tone of urgency.

Guidewords may also appear in two passages which are separated by a few or even many texts. When such appearances occur in previews or reviews, they function as framing devices. An example is the use of the word "hut" in 1:2–9 and 4:2–6, which draws all of 1:2—4:6 together into one compositional unit and supplies the lead theme; "The Future of the Deserted Hut." By the same token, the noun "vineyard" in 5:1–7 and 27:2–9 frames the first part of the book and supplies an element of its title: "The Vision of Ephraim's Fall and of David's Peaceable Vineyard" (5:1—27:13).

Still another example is the use of the word pair "new moon/sabbath" in 1:10–20 and 66:18–24, that is, at the beginning and at the end of Isa 1—66. Evidently, the pair highlights the compositional unity of the book. Similarly the word pair "heaven and earth" appears at the beginning of the book (1:2) and again at its conclusion, but now qualified by a telling adjective: "a new heaven and a new earth" (66:22).

"First and Second Isaiah"—Discourse and Source Analysis

How are the considerations presented so far related to the hypothesis that the book is the work of not one but two authors? Does the difference in perspective, style, and vocabulary between Isa 1—39 and 40—66 warrant positing a "Second Isaiah" as author of the second part?

If all of the large and many of the smaller sections have in fact the same thematic structure, it is reasonable to assume that the same mind which conceived the work in its entirety also shaped its individual sections and units. And since this guide is based on an approach akin to discourse analysis, it does not engage in genetic research, seeking to reconstruct the literary-historical stages of the work's presumed evolution. Further considerations are found in the discussion of "The Speaker" in the survey of the theology of Isa 1—66 below.

To be sure, discourse and source analysis neither exclude nor disqualify each other. They are different approaches and seek answers to different questions. Thus this preaching guide may profitably be used in conjunction with commentaries (see Bibliography) which are based on literary-historical or historical-critical approaches. Further comments are found below in the discussion of "The Speaker."

The Center and the Circle:
A Theology of Isaiah 1—66

A vision written is a vision made known. A vision made known seeks to enlighten and to persuade. Who are the persons to be enlightened, and by whom? How are they to be persuaded, and of what? The answers to these questions sketch a theology of the book.

First, the identity of the addressees: they are the remnant of Jacob-Israel who are loyal to the Lord and are called to bring back to the Lord not only their own people, but also people who hail from "all the ends of the earth" (45:22), heeding the invitation.

Second, the identity of the divinely commissioned messengers: they are disciples of Isaiah, son of Amoz, who embody through generations their master's teaching, live it out, and eventually mold it into the book called by his name.

Third, the manner of persuasion found in Isa 1—66: it is the literarily unfolded, cumulative argument that the Lord's rescues of Zion in the past establish the holy city's endurance as the center of worldwide Judaism.

Finally, the vision itself: it is the portrayal of a festive, law-observing city welcoming pilgrim and settler alike and sustaining the dispersed community of "the lovers of Zion" (66:10) with the Lord's instruction.

The Audience

"Come, House of Jacob, let us live in the Lord's light!" (2:5). Time and again the twelve tribes descended from Jacob-Israel are addressed, at first in their entirety, but soon only those who have escaped the Aramean-Ephraimite, Assyrian, and Babylonian attackers (4:2; 10:20–23; 14:1–2). That humble remnant (17:5–6; 37:30–32) is counseled to hide from the Lord's passing anger (26:20–21; 51:7–8) but also encouraged with words of comfort (40:1–2, 27–31; 41:8–16). Honored with the title "The Servant of the Lord," they are prepared for a mission to be carried out in patience, meekness, even pain (42:1–4; 49:3; 50:4–9). The task entrusted to the remnant-servant is first directed to the descendants of Jacob-Israel who are no longer loyal to the God of Israel but is then enlarged into an universal audience. The remnant is made nothing less than "a light to the peoples" and "a covenant of (the establishment of a new) nation" (49:1–13; 42:5–9).

Thus the remnant-servant Jacob-Israel reaches out to those who are sprung from Abraham and Sarah (51:1–3), but also to persons who cannot claim Abraham or Jacob as their father (63:7—64:11). As a result, descendants of Noah, "the nations," together with children of Isaac and Abraham, "the peoples," join in the acknowledgment that the remnant-servant's faithfully executed mission has brought him humiliation, suffering, even death, but brought them life and well-being (52:13—53:12).

All who are loyal to the Lord, whatever their parentage or status (56:3–8; 56:9—57:21), are transformed into a new Israel (43:1—44:8). They are re-created by the divine spirit (32:9–20; 31:1–3), reconciled to and feasting with each other (2:4; 11:6–8; 25:6–8), and are sheltered in a tabernacle of celestial glory (4:2–6). Wherever they may reside in the far-flung orbit of the Lord's earth, in Egypt or in Mesopotamia, in Canaan or in Mediterranean coastlands (40:22–24; 33:13–16; 19:24–25; 66:18–20), they come to Jerusalem as law-observant settlers and pilgrims. They are eager to be instructed by the Lord's priests, teachers, and judges (2:3; 66:10, 1–6) and to celebrate the festivals of Passover, Pentecost, and Tabernacles in "the city of our feasts" (33:20).

The Speaker

Who is the person credited with a vision of such breadth and depth, spanning more than two centuries from the reign of King Uzziah (786–742 B.C.E.; compare 1:1; 6:1) to that of the Persian emperor Cyrus (559–538 B.C.E.; compare 45:1–8)? His name is Isaiah, the son of Amoz (1:1; 13:1; 20:2; 37:2; 38:1). He is identified as "the prophet" in 37.3; 38:1; and 39:3, thus only in that part of the book which is identical with 2 Kings 18:13—20:19. This connects Isa 1—66 directly to the larger work of which it is now an integral part (see the discussion above).

In other words, the portrayal of the author-visionary, according to the central section (36:1—39:8), is that of the "prophet" who receives divine revelation "in a vision" (compare Num 12:6–8). It is Isaiah's role to speak as "the prophet" during the successive reigns of four Judaite kings in the second half of the eighth century B.C.E., just as it will be Jeremiah's role a century later (see Jer 1:1–3, 4–10, 11–19). The portrayal of Isaiah is thus an integral part of the book's message.

Accordingly, information is sparse concerning the person of the prophet but plentiful concerning his role. For instance, 8:1–4 tells of a (symbolic) name to be given a child yet to be born, of the prophet's impregnation of his wife, "the prophetess," and of the subsequent birth of a son who is given the already announced name. The passage concludes with an explanation of the child's name with reference to national events in the future. While the story portrays Isaiah as married and the father of a son, the narrative is interested in that information primarily for its symbolic significance. By the same token, the prophet's ready access to the king (7:1–17; 35:2–7; 38:1—39:8) may suggest that he belonged to the elite or held an office at the court. However, the passages that deal with encounters between king and prophet are cast into a literary mold which is typical of that of other such encounters told elsewhere in Scripture (compare 1 Kings 18:1–46 or Jer 36:1–32).

In keeping with this prophetic image, Isaiah not only mediates divine revelation into the terrestrial sphere, but also represents his people and its kings before their celestial lord. Thus he pleads on their behalf, agonizes over the ruin of Moab or Jerusalem, and calls them to remember divine mercies experienced in the past (6:1–13; 38:1–8; 15:5; 22:4; 63:7–14; compare 1 Kings 17:17–24; Jer 18:19–20; also Gen 20:7 and Num 12:13). In short, the presentation of Isaiah, man and prophet, is not so much biographical-historical as thematic-theological; the prophet and his disciples are first and foremost "signs and portents in Israel" (8:18–19).

How are Isaiah and his disciples pictured as "signs"? They are shown as (a) passionate advocates of their heavenly lord's superiority, (b) defying rejection by forming themselves into a living chain of successors through several generations, and (c) eventually committing their witness to writing.

Introduction   15

(a) Others may invoke the Lord's name but do so by rote and only with their lips, because their hearts are far from the divine (8:17; 28:7–13; 29:13; 30:9–11). Isaiah repeatedly and fervently argues the Lord's superiority over deities worshiped by Israel's neighbors and also by some members of Israel (40:12–26; 41:5–7; 44:9–20; 46:8–13). This is why the divine name YHWH (LORD in KJV, RSV, NEB, NJV, but "Yahweh" in JB) is in this prophet's word many times preceded by the vocative "my lord" (for instance 3:15; 7:7; 22:12; 28:16; 40:10; 56:8), showing that Isaiah and his followers know themselves set apart from those who do not in truth confess the Lord God of Israel as their divine master.

(b) It is the rejection of Isaiah's word which leads to the divinely ordered sealing of the prophet's testimony within the hearts of the individuals whom Isaiah calls "the children whom the Lord gave me" (8:18; compare 8:11–12). Thus a succession of prophets who cherish their master's instruction, pass it and its spirit from generation to generation, and claim for it nothing less than the role of "covenant" between the Lord and Israel (59:21; compare 48:16b; 63:7—65:25). The initially latent but then increasingly patent "vision of the whole" (29:11) illumines these disciples and prompts them to challenge their blind contemporaries to open eyes and minds (6:9–10; 29:10; 42:18–25; 61:1–3). Eventually the rebuilding of Zion, made possible after the (long announced) defeat of Babylon at the hands of the Medes (and Persians), visibly confirms that vision (44:24—45:13; 46:8–13; compare 14:22–23; 21:1–10).

(c) It is the literary unfolding of that vision which gives shape to the sizeable composition Isa 1—66, exceeded in volume among the prophetic books only by Jer 1—52. Its sustained and differentiated argument is discussed below. Suffice it to note that it is a work born of reflection and accordingly cast in visionary-meditative style. Prophetic passion and rational argument draw on hallowed tradition and inherited wisdom in order to create a work which contains both what is old and what is new. Thus the seer freely moves thematically from earth to heaven, from near to far, from past to future, and also from priest to prophet, from commoner to king, from male to female. The same freedom is evident in the use of literary devices: different images are readily juxtaposed, quotes aligned with quotes, prayers set next to reproaches, liturgies next to monologues, and scriptural allusion next to legal prescription.

In sum, the book was composed shortly after the rebuilding of the Jerusalem Temple in 520 B.C.E. Its authors were prophetic visionaries who responded to the new situation by casting their master's tradition into the sustained work which Isa 1—66 represents. They did so in accordance with the standard of prophetic legitimacy which characterizes the encyclopedic activity that gave birth to "A Book of Remembrance" (Genesis—Malachi, as found under the name "The Law and the Prophets" in the Hebrew Bible, see the discussion above). What the "historical" Isaiah had begun in due time found its literary expression in the disciples' work.

The Argumentation

How does the book present its case? What is the nature of its argumentation? It is persuasion—persuasion (1) supported by a parabolic composition found in the middle of the work, (b) buttressed by evidence with which the audience is familiar, and (c) clinched by an obvious, squarely visible proof.

(a) The prophet's "parable of the farmer" (28:23–29) shows that the Lord's "counsel" is indeed cause for wonder. Its thesis is presented in two paragraphs: (i) The farmer's preparation of the soil for seeding is a sequence of specific actions, each fully appropriate to its purpose: plowing the soil, opening seed furrows, selecting the proper seeds, and inserting them into the soil at locations suitable for their growth (24–25). (ii) Then, at harvest time, the farmer selects for each ripening fruit the fitting way of processing: he will neither run wagon wheels over cumin pods nor thresh wheat ears longer than needed (27–28; compare 5:1–7).

Thus, as goal orientation and labor differentiation characterize the work of the farmer, so "the work of the Lord" is a matter of long-range design and variety of methods. The divine plan may seem "strange," and its interpreters, the proph-

Introduction 17

ets, not welcome (28:21; 5:12), but once the "vision of the whole" (29:11) has given to the Lord's people new insight, past, present, and even future are seen as determined by the coherent pattern of divine purpose.

(b) What is the familiar evidence to which Isa 1—66 appeals? It is the miraculous rescue of Jerusalem twice within the span of the prophet's life: first from the attack of the Aramean-Ephramite coalition in 733 B.C.E. and then, a generation later, from the siege of the Assyrian army in 701 B.C.E. In both instances the enemy was militarily superior, in each case the continued existence of Jerusalem as the place of the Lord's presence threatened, yet both times the city was saved, as Isaiah had announced (7:1–17; 36:1—37:38). Hence, if such rescue has twice occurred in the past, well attested and prophetically foreseen, Isaiah's announcement of the Babylonians' fall is vindicated in advance as harbinger of Zion's rescue, though the city will have to endure humiliation, even physical destruction (2 Kings 25:1–21; Jer 39:1–9; 52:1–30). This argument, repeatedly advanced in 40:1—47:15, is summarized in 46:8–13: here the prophetic call turns the hearers' attention to "first things of old," that is, to the rescues of Jerusalem in the eighth century, as declared beforehand by the prophet. "From the start" the Lord has declared through Isaiah "the end," to be exact, the destruction of Babylon by the Medes (and Persians) under Cyrus (13:2—14:23; 21:1–10). That very king, appropriately honored with the title "the anointed of the Lord" (45:1), does give the order for Jerusalem's rebuilding, thus carrying out the divine plan (44:28; 45:10).

(c) Finally, what is the evidence which completes this argument? How is it clinched? It is the fact that the Temple in Jerusalem not only is rebuilt on highest orders but increasingly attracts worshipers from far and near (44:24–28; 49:14–26; 54:1–3; compare Jer 41:4–5). The latter is all the more surprising since the new building seemed "like nothing" to those who had seen it "in its former splendor" (Hag 2:2–5). Zion's rise after 520 B.C.E. to the status of cultic and legal center for the dispersed descendants of Jacob, Abraham, and Noah amazed pilgrim, settler, and resident alike (60:4–22; compare 43:5–7; 49:14–26; 54:1–3; 66:18–21). Thus the visionary exuberance of the book exceeds the sober realism of Haggai's words, seeking to attract and convince those whom it addresses.

The Vision of the Lord's Vineyard

What is the sum and substance of this prophetic vision? What are its major aspects and important elements? The reflective and wide-ranging style of the book presents a variety of images which describe aspects of its comprehensive perception. One guideword and image which stands out is that of "vineyard"—a word employed as guide- and frameword (see the discussion above and its occurrences in 1:2–9; 5:1–7; 27:2–9; and 65:21–23). Based on the notion of Israel as the Lord's vineyard, the following review of the vision's main features (1) describes the vineyard, then (b) turns to the people who are its keepers, and finally (c) shows how that vineyard is both the Lord's creation and re-creation.

(a) Unlike the Lord's vineyard described in the vineyard song as spoiled by its faithless keepers (5:1–7; 3:1—4:1), the restored vineyard is purified of idolatry and divinely protected, its vines deeply rooted and abundantly watered. At peace with its divine master and with itself, it reaches out and covers the world with its tendrils and its fruit (27:2–9; 2:2–4; 11:1–9). The communities of the loyal and observant, wherever they may reside, are equally its shareholders and are as pilgrim worshipers especially welcome in its center, the holy city (19:24–25; 33:13–16; 43:5–7). There they meet in mutual acceptance and in festive celebration, there they take for arbitration legal cases which cannot be settled at home, and there they hear teachers and preachers discourse on their common heritage (60:1–22; 58:1–14; 2:2–4; 4:2–6; 25:6–8; 30:19–26). Those who accept the invitation "to walk in the light of the Lord" (2:5) find long and weary journeys made easy and the hospitality of the mother city inviting (27:12–13; 35:8–10; 40:3–5; 43:1–7). They rest assured that their lands are part of the Lord's vineyard and their communities of faith, divinely provided "waters in the wilderness," blessed (43:20–21; compare 19:18–22).

(b) As Isaiah moves from its opening text units to its concluding ones, stern chastisements of the disloyal gradually give way to pleading invitations. Thus the first preview of the book (1:2—2:5) reprimands Israel's lack of loyalty generally (1:2-9) and faithlessness in cultic and social life specifically (1:10-31; compare 24:4-13). By comparison, the opening units of the third part (40—55) address with words of persuasion and consolation a disheartened and idolatry-prone Israel (40:1-31). The persons who have responded to the invitation, though only a remnant, are set apart to become restorers of the "vineyard." Their mission takes them first to Israel at large, then beyond (42:5-9; 49:1-13). Their task is a trying one, demanding gentle persistence and ready acceptance of instruction, but also endurance, humiliation, rejection, and suffering (42:1-4; 42:18—44:22; 50:4-11; 52:13—53:12). Yet eventually that mission is crowned with success: Israel is acknowledged as "priests of the Lord" (61:4-9; compare Exod 19:5-6), is secured by a perpetual, prophetically mediated covenant (49:8-13; 59:21), and is guided by the Lord's "anointed ones," whether royal or prophetic figures (45:1-8; 61:1-3; compare 9:1-6; 11:1-5; 32:9-20).

(c) The envisioned restoration of Israel transcends even the redemption from Egypt. It calls the new people of the Lord not only from one land but from everywhere, East or West, North or South. It brings them to the Lord's holy hill, not through hostile desert, but on easily traversed road. It invites them to a journey, not of trial and death, but of joy and singing (12:4-6; compare 11:11-16; 43:5-7; 40:3-5; 52:11-12; 55:12-13). The divine intervention creates, as it were, a new heaven and a new earth: Jerusalem, where the Lord's people worship at the high feasts and from whence they derive the assurance of blessing, well-being, and the Lord's prevenient grace (65:17-25; compare 66:22). Fittingly, Israel responds to its renewal, effected by the divine spirit, with "a new song," the hymn of the redeemed of the Lord (26:11-19; 32:9-20; 35:8-10; 42:10-12).

Preaching from Isaiah 1—66

In order to facilitate the use of this guide, at this point (1) the nature and arrangement of the exposition of each sermon text is explained, (2) recommended Bible translations are reviewed, and (3) themes and texts for sermons and sermon series are suggested.

The Use of the Guide

The individual expositions presented in the present guide briefly review the main features of the biblical passage (which is usually the length of a sermon text as found in lectionaries). Then one or two prominent motifs or themes in the passage are identified as possible sermon topics and discussed within the (narrower) context of the text itself and within the (wider) contexts of Isa 1—66, that is, the contexts of "The Law and the Prophets" and of the Bible as a whole. Isaiah's "vision of the whole" (29:11) is kept before the readers' eyes, counteracting the fragmentation of the biblical text to which a passage-by-passage interpretation easily falls prey. Hence what are offered here for persons preparing sermons are not outlines but starters, not mini-sermons but pointers and suggestions.

When readers review the Table of Contents, they are able to note at a glance how the sustained work is divided into parts, sections, segments, and sermon texts. It is of course not necessary to limit oneself to one such text—one may also use larger text units as the basis for a sermon. Moreover, in many cases the dividing line between the individual sermon texts is not a hard and fast one; there are many connections between texts which allow or suggest their juxtaposition for purposes of preaching. In fact, it is helpful and instructive to set different passages side by side and in this way capture some of the richness and texture of biblical literature. Hence the user is urged to look up the biblical cross-references.

Care has been taken to keep each exposition proportional to the length of the biblical passage, thus ensuring for seemingly less interesting passages at least some hearing. Occasionally the exposition will discuss troublesome notions which appear in the text, to be acknowledged and considered if preaching is not to evade sensitive issues (see, for example, 34:1–17).

Furthermore, several texts are discussed in the Introduction (see, for example, 28:23-29); reference to it will enrich the readers' appreciation of many a passage. Finally, references to early Christian writings (NT), and occasionally also to those of early rabbinic Judaism, show how an Isaianic/biblical theme made its impact on these works.

Recommended Translations

As a rule, preachers gain more from a biblical passage when they read it in several translations and compare the various renderings. The most recent translation of "The Prophets" is the New Jewish Version (NJV), published by the Jewish Publication Society in 1978. It is highly recommended, though the user will find that in quite a few passages the translation committee could not arrive at a consensus and therefore either noted that the "Hebrew is uncertain" or resorted to emendations. The older Jewish version of the Hebrew Bible, published in one volume in 1917 by the same publisher, is still very serviceable.

Among Christian Bibles, the (essentially Protestant and North American) Revised Standard Version (RSV), the (essentially Protestant and British) New English Bible (NEB), and the (original French Roman Catholic) Jerusalem Bible (JB) are recommended. These Bible editions are the work of scholarly teams and endorsed by churches, hence preferable to translations or paraphrases done by one person. The latter may profitably be used, however, in conjunction with those mentioned first. The Good News Bible is published by the Bible Society and employs simple vocabulary; as such it is a valuable resource. Finally, for the rendering of poetic passages (and Isaiah is mostly in poetic form) the King James Version (KJV) remains important.

Sermon Suggestions

The preparation of sermons is in a special way the responsibility of ordained persons. In several communions a lectionary prescribes liturgical readings and with them biblical passages on which sermons should be based. In other churches, preachers are free to choose topics and texts.

Whatever the principle of text selection, this guide is offered as a new resource. For individual sermons on a text in Isaiah, the expositions present suggestions and points to be pondered. For more sustained preaching on Isaiah, possible series of sermons are recommended, which would explore the book in a fuller and more differentiated manner. Five such series are suggested below: a series may (a) follow the liturgical year, or deal with such broad topics as (b) "Pilgrimage to Peace," (c) "The Wonder of Renewal," or (d) "The Inclusive View." A sermon series might also explore (e) "The Work of Jesus in Isaiah's Words."

FROM EXPECTATION TO FULFILLMENT (see Isa 46:3–4)
Preaching from the Book of Isaiah
Through the Liturgical Year

11:1–9 and 25:6–8	Expectation	Advent
7:10–19 and 9:1–6	Celebration	Christmas
49:1–13 and 60:1–22	Proclamation	Epiphany
14:1–2 and 58:1–14	Contrition	Ash Wednesday
1:10–20 and 59:1–21	Penitence	Lent
43:1–13 and 66:18–24	Pilgrimage	Palm Sunday
42:1–4 and 50:4–11	Suffering	Good Friday
35:1–10 and 43:23	Praise	Easter
32:9–20 and 61:1–3	Mission	Pentecost
43:16–28 and 65:17–20	Consummation	Trinity Season

PILGRIMAGE TO PEACE (see Isa 52:7–10)

57:14–21 and 33:13–16	The Road to Peace
5:1–7 and 27:2–9	The Reign of Peace
2:1–5 and 61:1–3	The Season of Peace
8:23b—9:6 and 11:1–9	The Fruits of Peace

THE WONDER OF RENEWAL (see Isa 32:15–20)

1:2–9 and 28:23–29	Divine Patience
26:11–19 and 25:6–8	Death's Defeat
32:9–20 and 61:1–3	Spirit's Work
65:17–20 and 66:22–24	New Creation

THE INCLUSIVE VIEW (see Isa 29:9–14)

2:1–5 and 19:24–25	Israel, Assyria, and Egypt
3:16—4:1 and 51:1–3	Sarah and Abraham
56:1–8 and 63:15—64:11	Proselytes and Disenfranchised
43:1–7 and 11:1–9	Adversaries and Friends

THE WORK OF JESUS IN ISAIAH'S WORDS
(see Luke 4:16–21)

Matt 1:18–25	Isa 7:1–17; 9:1–6	Births of Emmanuel
Mark 4:3–20	Isa 6:9–10; 29:9–14	Mysteries of the Kingdom
Luke 4:16–21	Isa 61:1–3; 8:11–23	Powers of the Spirit
John 1:19–23	Isa 40:3–5; 41:17–20	Voices from the Wilderness
John 4:20–24	Isa 66:1–6; 40:12–26	Worship in Spirit
Acts 8:26–39	Isa 52:13—53:12; 50:4–9	Suffering Servants

1 Cor 15:50–58	Isa 25:6–8; 65:17–20	Conquests of Death
Eph 2:11–22	Isa 57:14–21; 19:24–25	Reconciliations
Heb 2:10–15	Isa 8:11–23; 59:21	Prophetic Mediations
James 3:13–18	Isa 32:9–20; 40:6–8	Descents of Wisdom
1 Peter 2:1–10	Isa 28:14–22; 54:11–17	Cornerstones of Faith
Rev 21:1–7	Isa 65:17–20; 4:2–6	New Creations

The Title of the Book: The Vision of Isaiah
(Isaiah 1:1)

The opening verse, like the front page of a modern book, supplies summary information in light of which readers and hearers are asked to receive the work. According to it, the composition which now begins puts into literary form what a named person received through a vision during a certain period of time and relating to a named city and an identified nation.

As a vision, Isa 1—66 is that medium of revelation which according to "The Law of Moses" (Genesis–Deuteronomy) is appropriate for the prophets of the Lord God of Israel. Only Moses, son of Amran, is privileged to see and encounter the God of Israel "face to face" and speak with the divine "plainly, mouth to mouth," while to the prophets of Israel and Judah God grants revelation "in a vision" or "in a dream" (Deut 34:10; Num 12:6).

Thus the prophets' relation to their God is less direct and immediate in comparison to that of the archprophet Moses, but it is real, direct, and privileged nevertheless. It empowers them to perceive what is made known to them with their mental eye and then to speak of it in ways no other human beings can. By the same token, the prophets' less direct, visionary relation to the Lord subordinates their words to those of Moses. The words of the latter have been put into writing in what is the first and foremost part of the Hebrew Scriptures. "The Law of Moses" thus precedes and subordinates to itself all that follows it within the confines of the Scriptures, including the words of the prophets.

It follows that the identification of Isa 1—66 as "a vision" makes this book an integral part of the ongoing self-disclosure of the Lord to those who have eyes to see, fitting it like a link into the chain of divine revelation to Israel and to its spiritual heirs (see the Introduction for a fuller discussion of the relation of Isaiah to "The Law and the Prophets").

The name of the visionary is Isaiah, son of Amoz. His father's name is thus different from that of one of the prophets among "The Twelve Minor Prophets," Amos of Tekoa. Isaiah's name appears in the Hebrew Bible only in 2 Kings and its 2 Chronicles parallels, that is, only in those passages which are identical with Isa 36—39. Etymologically, the name means "The Lord rescues." And since the divine rescue theme is central in Isaiah, the name may be understood as symbolic—all the more so because symbolic names are a prominent feature of the book (compare 7:3, 14, and 8:1).

While post-biblical legends tell of Isaiah's ascension into the seventh heaven as well as of his martyrdom and thus attest interest in him as a holy man, the biblical book bearing his name has little to say about his person but much about his prophetic role. Generations of followers, persuaded that his visionary eye had seen in advance the trials they themselves were encountering, eventually gave shape to a book bearing his name. It affirms that Jerusalem's memorable escapes from first Aramean-Ephraimite, then Asyrian, threats of conquest and occupation (7:1—8:10; 36:1—37:38) are reassuring harbingers of the future rescue of the holy city from the looming threat of extinction by the Babylonians.

The headline relates Isaiah's visionary activity to the reigns of four successive Judaite kings: Uzziah (783–742 B.C.E.), Jotham (742–735 B.C.E.), Ahaz (735–715 B.C.E.), and Hezekiah (715–687 B.C.E.). However, 6:1–13 and 36:1—37:38 may be taken to indicate that the prophet's prophetic activity began only in Uzziah's last year (742 B.C.E.) and ended soon after Sennacherib's withdrawal from Jerusalem (701 B.C.E.). It is not certain, though, whether the commissioning of the prophet with words of doom for his people as narrated in 6:1–13 should be understood as reference to the inception of his prophetic activity generally.

It is noteworthy that the listing of the four successive reigns of Judaite kings in 1:1, at the beginning of the series of three prophetic books which came to be called "The Major Prophets" (Isaiah–Jeremiah–Ezekiel), is paralleled in form and substance in Hos 1:1, the beginning of a similar series of prophetic books, that is, "The Twelve Minor Prophets." In both series the listing of the first prophet's period of activity is continued within the series (see Jer 1:1–3 and Ezek 1:2–3 on the one hand, and Amos 1:1; Mic 1:1; Zeph 1:1; Hag 1:1; and Zech 1:1 on the other). This correspondence suggests that the two series of prophetic books balance and complement each other. In other words, the series Isaiah–Jeremiah–Ezekiel contains prophetic words primarily spoken to "Judah and Jerusalem" (Isa 1:1), and the series Hosea–Malachi primarily addresses Israel at large (compare Hos 1:2—3:5, which functions as prologue to "The Twelve Minor Prophets"). This observation also explains the inversion of the two series of prophetic books in the Greek Bible (Septuagint), where Hosea–Malachi precedes Isaiah–Ezekiel. Evidently the Greek-speaking descendants of Jacob-Israel stressed their common and more inclusive descent from Jacob and so placed the words spoken to all of Jacob's descendants (Hosea–Malachi) first in their Bible editions, followed by prophetic books specifically addressed to Judah and Jerusalem (Isaiah–Ezekiel).

In sum, the preacher notes that the seemingly dry and technical statistics of the book's headline open a wide horizon as well as provide a key to what follows in the book itself.

Prologue: The Future of the Deserted City
(Isaiah 1:2—4:6)

The prologue condenses the book's dominant theme sequence "castigation–consolation" into near polarity and proceeds to present it in two parallel sections: 1:2—2:5 and 2:5—4:6 (see the Introduction, "Thematic Structure"). Both sections move from reproach (1:2—20; 2:6—4:1) to promise (1:21—2:4; 4:2–6); they are linked by a hinge-like invitation to Israel "to walk in the Lord's light" (2:5). The sections thus serve as a doubled preview of the entire book; as such they provide the perspective in which its audience is directed to read all that follows.

The Exaltation of Apostate Zion (1:2—2:5)

The first of the two sections is made up of two chastisements (1:2–9, 10–20), two promises (1:21–31; 2:1–4), and a summons (2:5).

The Miracle of a Remnant (1:2–9)

The narrative framing of dialogue is a common literary feature of the Scriptures. Here the prophet's chastisement (4–8) is introduced by the quotation of a divine reprimand (2b–3) and followed by the people's acceptance of both (9).

The prophet recites for all to hear the Lord's assertion of the people's failure to live in filial obedience, then describes its lamentable result: comparable to a person wounded from head to toe yet not cared for and bound up, Israel finds its land laid waste, its cities burnt, and its labors come to no fruition. Its capital city is left deserted, "like a hut in a vineyard." It is a miracle that there are a few who have survived—and that is acknowledged as the work of the Lord.

A sermon may explore the notion of the remnant. After all, does not Deut 21:18–21 decree that persistently disobedient sons are to be removed from the community and stoned? Should the divine response to Israel's disloyalty not be the same as it had been to Sodom's and Gomorrah's obstinacy (Gen 18:1—19:29)? What makes the difference here as elsewhere in Isa 1—66 is the small number of those who escape through divine intervention (6:12–13; 7:1–9; 37:30–32). These faithful people are set apart to become the Lord's servants and to act as the restorers of ruined vineyard and deserted hut (40:27–31; 42:5–9).

The two guidewords "vineyard" and "hut" (a shelter in the open field for persons guarding the ripening fruits, as well as the booth used ritually at the Feast of Tabernacles) appear side by side and in this way set a thematic stage for the entire book (see the discussion of guide- and framewords in the Introduction). In short, 1:2–9 introduces a master theme, that of "vineyard and festive city"—a double motif which is important also in the NT (see John 15:1–8; Luke 2:41–51). It is within that setting that the remnant motif introduces both divine judgment and mercy.

The Peril of Selective Obedience (1:10–20)

The Lord's people may escape the fate of Sodom and Gomorrah but not the castigation due to those who act like the two defiant cities. The divine words conveyed by the prophet pound the hearers like waves; in terse phrase after phrase the prophet first rejects in the Lord's name the many rituals observed by the people (11–15), then pleads for a change (16–18), and finally presents the choice between life and death (19–20). The Lord's response sarcastically takes up the people's reference to Sodom and Gomorrah (1:9) by applying it to them, "You rulers of Sodom, you people of Gomorrah, do listen!"

The list of acts of worship carried out within the confines of the Jerusalem Temple is comprehensive. They range from sacrifices such as burnt offerings to observances of holy seasons such as the sabbath to expressions of personal piety such as prayers. What makes these prescribed obligations unacceptable is the worshipers' failure to observe equally commanded social obligations, especially actions in accord with the standards of justice laid out in "The Law of Moses." Does it not demand as much kindness to one's fellow human beings as service to the Lord? More specifically, does not Moses' summary of the divine legislation, promulgated shortly before his death (Deut 1:6—30:20), stress the importance of uniformly observed norms in legal, social, and ritual observances (compare Deut 16:18–20)? Does it not exhort Israel to be considerate of the disadvantaged, such as widows and orphans (Deut 24:17–22; 27:19), and warn against shedding innocent blood by not following the stipulated procedures in capital cases (see Deut 17:8–13; 19:1–21; 27:25)?

Preaching on the peril of selective obedience invites the congregation to another chance: "Come now, let us reason together!" The divine imperative is, after all, not arbitrary. The Lord's law, when faithfully observed by Israel, is admired by the nations: do they not acknowledge both Israel's discernment and the law's perfection (Deut 4:5–8)? Observance of the law is indeed a matter of will and decision.

Thus Isaiah, the prophet legitimated by the standard of the Law of Moses, confronts his hearers with the same alternative as does the lawgiver: Life or Death (compare 1:19–20 with Deut 30:15–21). Once the choice for life has been made, the coming of the Lord's worshipers to the Temple on Mount Zion becomes a new lease on life, the celebration of holy seasons in its precincts, a banquet of joy and the meeting with festive crowds, an assurance of their worldwide communion in the knowledge of the Lord (2:2–5; 11:9; 25:6–8; 65:17–20). Then, figuratively speaking, red does indeed become white; a sabbath rejected is transformed into a sabbath accepted (1:18, compare 58:13–14; 66:22–24).

The Certainty of Refinement (1:21–31)

Silver turned into dross, wine adulterated with water—such is the prophet's lament over what has befallen Jerusalem. Acceptance of bribes and disregard for the disadvantaged have become standard practice and have turned the once observant city into its opposite (21–23). The divine response, however, is not acquiescence. As precious metal is purified by smelting out impurities, so Jerusalem will be cleansed: the Lord will give to her law-observing leadership "as at first" (he did when choosing David; 24–26) but will bring the practices of apostates to a shameful end (29–31). Zion's ultimate triumph will be achieved "through loyalty to the Lord," while deserters will disappear (27–28). The description of Jerusalem as "harlot" is more than colorful language: in the prophet's time fertility rites carried out at the Temple seem to have included sacred prostitution, a practice not abolished until a century after Isaiah's lifetime (2 Kings 23:7). Moreover, certain rites associated with "high mountains," "gardens," and "trees" were also acts of apostasy (57:7; 66:15–17; compare Deut 12:2–3). On the other hand, the Lord's restoration of Zion will turn it into a garden comparable to Paradise, elevated so that it is higher than all other mountains, well watered and treed (compare 30b with 65:17–23; 2:2; 30:25; and 55:12–13).

Sermons at times gild the past at the expense of the present; this passage does so with good warrant. Is not the reign of King David, who captured Jerusalem from the Canaanites, made it his kingdom's capital, and ruled from there, described as execution of "true justice among all the people" (2 Sam 8:13; 22:22–28; 23:1–7)? No one among the kings succeeding David in Jerusalem, with the exception of Hezekiah and Josiah, is so distinguished. On the contrary, they fail to abide by their forefather's standards and tolerate old or even introduce new apostasies (see 1 Kings 14:21–24; 2 Kings 14:1–6).

But during Isaiah's lifetime King Hezekiah (and King Josiah a century later) fully measures up to David, as does Zerubbabel, governor of Judah under the Persians and descendant of David (2 Kings 18:3–7; 22:2; Hag 1:12–13; 2:20–23), at the end of the Babylonian exile. Through them the Lord indeed restores to Jerusalem "counselors as at first" and thus is able to honor her with the title "loyal city" (26). In sum, Jerusalem's future restoration under Hezekiah and Josiah is harbinger of still greater things to come: initiated by Zerubbabel, Zion will become the center of worldwide Israel, a pilgrimage center inviting not only Jacob's descendants, but also the sons and daughters of Isaac and Rebecah, of Abraham and Sarah, and even of Noah (2:1–5).

The Future of Zion's Peace (2:1–4)

"Swords into plowshares" has become one of the best known biblical calls to action. The announcement to which it belongs (2–4) is introduced as "the word which Isaiah . . . saw concerning Judah and Jerusalem" (1), thus raising it above the status of a (mere) vision and giving it almost the authority of "the word of the Lord" communicated to the archprophet Moses without the medium of the vision (compare 6:1–13; Num 12:6–8; Deut 34:10). In this manner the annunciation of Zion's future is made the climax of 1:2—2:4, the first of the two previews of the entire book.

Surprising images capture the readers' imagination: the "end of days," the elevation of Mount Zion to a height above its surrounding hills, the coming of great crowds to a city located in relative obscurity, the adjudication of legal cases exclusively in Zion, the reforging of war implements into farming tools, and, finally, the termination of hostility among Abraham's and Sarah's many descendants, notably those alienated from each other, such as Ishmael and Isaac, Esau and Jacob, Judah and Joseph (2–4). Furthermore, the concluding invitation to the twelve tribes transforms this amazing collage into present privilege: pilgrims, settlers, and residents alike discover each other in the bazaars of Jerusalem and the courts of its Temple as members of one, worldwide community.

Each image can become a sermon starter. The transformation of history's goal into today's imperative makes pilgrimage to the holy city a celebration of new life (60:1–22; 65:15–25; 66:18–24; compare 1 Kings 8:27–53; Luke 2:41–51; Acts 2:1–13). The reach beyond the tribes of Jacob-Israel to the offspring of Abraham and Noah transcends the particularity of one people, including all human families among the Lord's servants (14:1–2; 25:6–8; 49:1–13; 56:9—57:21; compare Deut 23:8–9 and Acts 11:1–18). As proselyte or Godfearer, all women and men, whatever their pedigrees, are welcome and may claim their place in the worldwide community of Israel. Moreover, the centralized (and hence more uniform) adjudication of legal cases promotes harmony and cohesion (42:1–4; 51:1–8; compare 1:10–20; 5:24; 30:9–11; also Deut 17:8–13 and Acts 15:1–29), and the mutual understanding which the interaction with fellow pilgrims, residents, or new settlers fosters is an effective antidote to intertribal contention and strife (4:2–6; 11:9; 54:1–3; Ps 133; also Gal 3:28).

The almost word-for-word replication of Isa 2:2–4 in Mic 4:1–4 is unusual. The latter is part of the last "book" of "The Prophets," that is, of "The Twelve Minor Prophets." Thus, the doubled visionary word concerning the future of Zion's peace almost frames the prophetic writings. As bracket it elevates the peace-creating function of the holy city to that of "The Law of Moses"—note, for instance, the final petition of the "Aaronide Blessing:" it is for the gift of peace (Num 6:24–26).

By the same token, this thematic frame also encloses a passage which inverts a part of the call to peaceful coexistence: "Beat your plowshares into swords, and your pruning hooks into spears!" (Joel 4:10; compare 1–21). On the one hand, the contrast reminds readers and hearers of the continuing existence of both war and peace, but on the other hand, the framelike double occurrence of the inclusive vision of peace and well-being neutralizes, as it were, its antithesis and does not allow it to stand as the last word.

New Lease on an Ancient Shelter (2:5—4:6)

The section is linked to the preceding one by an invitation (2:5); it is made up of one general and two specific castigations (2:6–22; 3:1–15; 3:16—4:1) and concluded by a promise (4:2–6).

Reversals of Perspective (2:6-22)

Refrains not only create strophes but also identify lead themes. This unit is structured by two refrains. The first contrasts human abasement with the Lord's exclusive exaltation (11-17) and coordinates two strophes which deal with this theme (6b–11, 12–17). The second (19b–21b) describes divine intervention as cause for despair about human-made idols and juxtaposes two strophes (18–19, 20–21). Introduction (6a) and conclusion (22), both brief, frame the composition.

A further stylistic feature worth noting is the use of three guidewords: "Adam" (human beings in so far as Adam, who was granted divine breath, is their father; compare Gen 2:7) occurs five times, "nothings" (a derisive reference to images of the divine which are created by human effort) appears four times, and the adjective/noun "all" is employed no fewer than ten times. In short, already word choice and mode of composition indicate that the passage is comprehensive in approach and theological-reflective in perspective.

The preacher notes the same broad, meditative character in the text's argumentation. The first strophe throws its net wide, condemning mantic practices introduced from lands to the East and West, inordinate accumulation of wealth, horses, and chariots, and devotion to idols (compare Deut 18:10, 14; 17:16–17; 4:15–18). The second strophe seeks to include "all that is high and lifted up" and uses parabolic language as well: towering trees and lofty mountains, powerful fortifications and oceangoing vessels are listed as targets of "the Day of the Lord" (compare Amos 5:18–20).

The third and fourth strophes describe the results of the reversals: the deposit of idols in caves by the keepers, demonstrating the weakness of both. But the conclusion calls in a compassionate tone and with words of the Paradise story (Gen 2:7; compare 2:4b—3:24) for the recognition of human creatureliness and its dependency on the divine.

The preacher notes the stark contrast between the divine and the human spheres which Isa 1—66 generally posits, summed up elsewhere in the observation that those who are not loyal to the Lord rely on "flesh, not spirit" (31:3). The disparity relates to the physical and spiritual aspects of life; it also manifests itself concretely at various times and in different places. Do not Hezekiah and Josiah, two loyal kings of Judah, reverse the prevailing standards and therefore receive praise as princes of peace and counselors in the Lord's fear (compare 9:5–6 and 11:1–9 with 2 Kings 18:3–7a and 22:2)? Do not proud Assyria and Babylonia find themselves brought low and eventually defeated (compare 10:7–11; 14:12–23, 24–27; and 47:1–15 with 2 Kings 18:35 and Jer 50:2–3)? Moreover, does not divine intervention invert at times all human positions into their opposite, making priest like layman, and mistress like handmaid (24:1–3)?

The divinely caused upset equally affects religious rites and practices. Trusted images of the divine are thrown into crevices, their futility proven by their powerlessness to intervene on their devotees' behalf (18–21; compare 31:6–7; 44:21–22). Those who choose to ignore such upheavals fail to perceive that "the Day of the Lord" is at hand; they are engaged in revelry in the same manner in which Jerusalem is busy celebrating, when in fact a siege threatens (22:1–14; compare 13:2–22). The point is this: reversals in human affairs may call forth a response of resignation—or no response at all. But persons who are open to receive insight are transformed by the unexpected: "See, I am doing a new thing! Now it is about to appear—do you not recognize it?" (43:19a).

The Dishonor of Judah's Men (3:1–15)

Women disgraced and men dishonored—the complementary themes of 3:16—4:1 and 3:1–15 unfold in detail the theme of radical reversal which 2:6–22 has introduced. The elite of Jerusalem and Judah are singled out in both units. The first addresses men, the second turns to women. Both contain detailed lists: one, of some eleven different officeholders who will be removed from their positions (3:2–3), the other, of some twenty-one (!) items of feminine adornment which will be taken away (3:18–23).

Furthermore, in both passages a dramatic episode illustrates the despair of the deprived: there are two vignettes, one of a man and one of seven women each searching for protection after having lost everything but searching in vain (3:5–7; 3:25—4:1). In short, the stylistic parallelism shows that the twin units deal concretely with the reversal of human fate. The meditative mode of composition gives the prophet freedom to move back and forth between reflective argument (1–3, 8–9a), quotation of divine words (4, 12–15), exclamation (9b–11), and narrative (5–7).

The tradition about two Babylonian attacks (597 and 587 B.C.E.) and the earlier Assyrian siege (701 B.C.E.), as attested in Kings, supplies the motifs of a famine fateful for the besieged city (2 Kings 25:3), of exile or slaughter of the elite (2 Kings 24:15–16; 25:18–21), and of the misery of those left in the devastated land (2 Kings 24:17; 25:12, 22–26). The text also identifies the cause of the upset: the practice of partiality in legal proceedings and abusive bail setting (compare Deut 16:19–20 and Lev 5:20–26). Thus, Jerusalem's leaders are castigated as misleaders whose condemnation is sure (compare 2 Kings 23:26–27 and Jer 44:2–6).

To the preacher the passage suggests the theme of obligation: those holding positions of public trust are held responsible. The text specifically addresses "elders and administrators" (14), evidently reflecting offices of responsibility which began to evolve in the congregations of worldwide Judaism ("elder" corresponds to the Greek-derived "presbyter," which was an important position not only in ancient Israel and early Judaism, but also in the early churches).

The text refers to persons who are charged to make their people "go the right way" (13) yet are "ravaging the vineyard" (14). This accusation relates their action to the guideword "vineyard" which appears at the beginning, in the middle, and at the end of the book (see the discussion of guide- and framewords in the Introduction). Thus the passage relates itself to a master theme in Isa 1—66—that of the far-flung vineyard community of Israel. The image has remained an important one for the church, as the parable of the vineyard keepers (Mark 12:1–12) and the discourse on the true vine and its branches (John 15:1–8) show.

The Disgrace of Zion's Women (3:16—4:1)

Veils and mirrors, lace gowns and nose rings—the long list of items enjoyed by Jerusalem's privileged ladies makes for a unique text! However, the passage fits into the theme of 2:6—4:6, the second preview of the entire book. It moves from chastisement to promise, highlighting the motif of the divine reversal of all human affairs. While that notion is summarily unfolded in 2:6–22, the two units which follow go into detail in a parallel manner: the first addresses Judah's leading men, the second turns to its elite women.

First, the mincing gait and provocative comportment of the "daughters of Zion" are described, and their arrogance condemned. Then a great variety of jewelry and clothing, worn by the wives of the nation's aristocracy, is detailed item by item. However, their wealth and its display is of no avail when the great reversal of their status catches up with them. To drive home the point, the prophet sketches the frantic search of seven war widows for a male who is prepared to be their nominal husband and protector, though they themselves will supply their own needs. In sum, the passage paints with broad, grim strokes.

The preacher recognizes that this condemnation of female pride does not single out women in a manner substantially different from the way in which males are castigated in the preceding passage. Rather, the divinely caused reversal of all human presumption is the dominant theme—hence the preposition "instead of" appears no fewer than five times (3:24)! In its negative formulation the unit provides the dark background against which the positive descriptions of the coming restoration stand out. For instance, in 32:9–19 the appeal to "the carefree women" to lament the coming disaster is followed by the announcement of a spirit-mediated transformation into "calm and confidence for ever" (compare 4:4–6).

By the same token, in 61:1–3 the prophet formulates a pun to announce that the Lord will give to Zion instead of ashes (*'eper*) a headdress of honor (*pe'er*), using the very word "headdress" which according to 3:30 Zion's arrogant daughters had forfeited (*pe'erim*)! While defeated Babylon, pictured as a disgraced woman, must accept the reversal of her fate, restored Zion will "wear" her returned children "like a bride her finery" (47:1–15; 49:18). In short, the reversal theme informs this as many other texts in Isa 1—66.

The Transformation of Mount Zion (4:2–6)

Image crowds image, and each highlights a theme of purification and restoration. What awaits the residents and visitors of the holy city is the fertility of the land, remnant though they are. Their devotion to the Lord makes them choose life over death; hallowed to the God of Israel, they are "inscribed for ever in Jerusalem" (compare 44:1–5 and Deut 30:15–20). Purified and honored, the remnant find spiritual sustenance and physical safety in Zion. Day and night they are enlightened by the divine presence, sheltered forever against threats and temptations of apostasy (compare 61:19–20 and 25:1–5)—exuberant language indeed, fitting as a final affirmation of the book's preview and echoing conclusions of various parts and sections of the book itself (see 12:1–6; 27:12–13; 35:1–10; 48:20–22; 55:12–13; 66:22–23).

A sermon may explore the various images which the text offers. For instance, there is the celebration of the imminent glorification of Jerusalem through the arrival of many pilgrims and settlers (an Epiphany theme; compare 48:20–21; 60:1–22; 66:18–21), or the change of the ashes of humiliation into garments of honor (a Lent / Easter theme; compare 61:1–3), or the notion of the spirit-wrought new creation which affirms and transcends the old (a Pentecost theme; compare 32:9–20; 65:15–25; also Exod 13:21–22 and 40:33b–34).

On the other hand, the preacher may reflect on the guide-word "hut/booth" which frames the book's prologue (1:2—4:6). That which at the beginning is described in despair as "a deserted hut in a vineyard" (1:8) is at the end portrayed as "shade from heat and refuge from torrents" (4:6). Moreover, corresponding to the motif of the first forsaken, then restored "hut/booth," the prologue anticipates a parallel but broader poetic-prophetic exposition: that of the vineyard theme. Indeed, the first part of the book which now follows opens with that very motif: the song of the vineyard (5:1–7).

PART I
The Vision of Israel's Future and of Its Peaceable Mountain
(Isaiah 5:1—27:13)

This part is, like the two others (28—37 and 38—55), made up of two sections (5:1—12:6 and 13:1—27:13), each of which moves thematically from castigation through challenge to promise. The chastisement is addressed to "the House of Israel," specifically to Ephraim and Judah (5:7; 9:7). The primary challenge is Ephraim's attack on Judah (7:1–17; 9:17–20; 22:1–14). The promise is expressed in several ways: in the celebration of King Hezekiah's birth (9:1–6), in the vision of King Josiah's exemplary loyalty to the Lord's law (11:1–6; contrast 7:10–17), and in an announcement of a future banquet on Mount Zion for all peoples (25:6–8).

The Deserted Vineyard and the Shoot of Jesse (5:1—12:6)

The section comprises two segments: Isaiah's mandate in the vineyard (5:1—9:6) and the prophet's vision of peace (9:7—12:6).

Isaiah's Mandate in the Lord's Vineyard (5:1—9:6)

Against the sinister backdrop of Israel's failure (5:1-30), the vision of the divine mandate (6:1-13) sets the stage for the challenge to Jerusalem and Judah by Ephraim allied with Aram (7:1–8:10). The people's rejection of the Lord's chastisement through that attack eventually leads to the separation of Isaiah and his disciples from that disobedient people (8:11–23), but also to the announcement of the birth of a royal bearer of divine peace (9:1–6).

The Desertion of the Choice Vineyard (5:1–7)

The song of the carefully tended but fruitless vineyard is a parable. As such it teases its audience into reflection—a reflection they would rather not undertake. Engagingly beginning with the description of a familiar viticultural scene, it quickly captures the hearers' attention and carries them along with ease—until they find themselves confronted by a jarring turn, which changes the narrative mood and throws out a challenge. The switch from one mode of speaking to another gives the parable its peculiar punch and makes it memorable (compare a similar sudden change in Nathan's parable of the ewe lamb told to King David after his adultery with Bathsheba [2 Sam 12:1–6], or the parable of the vineyard keepers which Mark's Jesus tells [Mark 12:1–11]).

Parables are born of the reflection which crystallizes into the larger work of which they are parts; hence they move within the conceptual horizon of that larger work and provide focal points for the reflection of the audience on the theme which the composition in its entirety presents. The vineyard song 5:1–7 condenses the prophet's conviction that the people do not respond in gratitude to its divine lord into a strong opener for the book's first part (5:1–27:13), the very part which concludes with the call to celebrate the restored vineyard and its holy mountain (27:2–13).

A sermon may pursue the "vineyard" motif from the book's beginning (1:8; 3:13–15), through its framing role in the first part, to allusions in a negative mode (36:17) as well as in a positive one (65:21). It may then explore other vineyard parables such as the narrative of the unjustly and the justly expelled vineyard keepers (1 Kings 21:1–29; Mark 12:1–11). In the song itself the description of the Lord's successive actions of care for the vineyard points to aspects of divine providence for Israel, such as the gift of the Land of Canaan, a land flowing with milk and honey (5:1; compare Exod 3:8), the planting of the people in that land (5:20; compare Exod 15:17a), the erection of a central shelter within it (5:2a; compare Exod 15:17b), and the expectation of a positive response from the people (5:2b; compare Exod 19:5–6).

A homily may also deal with the theme of foiled expectation. This is expressed in the Hebrew text by two puns which NJV imitates: the Lord "hoped for justice, but behold, injustice; for equity, but behold, iniquity" (5:7). The cause of the Lord's disappointed hope is described in Isaiah in a variety of ways: children not turning out (1:2–3), men and women betraying trust (3:1—4:1), and a people turning against itself (9:17–20). However, the announcement of the divine restoration knows not only of a new vineyard, but also, again expressed in a pun, of exaltation instead of exasperation (61:3).

The Desertion of the Lord's Word (5:8–30)

"Woe to those who . . . !" Stern condemnations of injustice and arrogance, of idolatry and apostasy, of pride and licentiousness ring through many a biblical text—and many a sermon since! In this passage, six strophes of varying length (8–11, 11–17, 18–19, 20, 21, 22–23) detail actions which illustrate the inversion of equity into iniquity, a notion introduced by the preceding vineyard parable (5:7) and summarily described in 5:24b as contempt for both the letter and the spirit of the Lord's law. Attitude and actions born of apostasy are interpreted as the reason for the continuing divine anger; it expresses itself in the assault of the seemingly invincible Assyrian attackers (25a, 26–30), burning up land and people like fire devouring straw (24a).

The preacher notes that the series of six "woe!" texts has a counterpart in a more extended sequence of six "woe!" strophes in the book's second part (28:1—33:9). They are each introduced by the same exclamation of lament and sorrow, thus linking the two parts of the book and in this way, as it were, paralleling the Aramean-Ephraimite and Assyrian threats of Judah's existence.

On the other hand, that second series quickly leads to a different conclusion: the succeeding texts (33:10—35:10) announce disaster to the nations, notably those allied with Assyria, but restoration to Israel and Zion. Not so in 5:8–23! Here the succeeding texts show how far the people of the Lord have removed themselves from the divine presence: two disasters overtake them (6:12–13), because leader and people do not rely on the Lord (7:1—8:10). Eventually the prophet is ordered to separate himself with his disciples from that people (8:11–23). The last word of 5:1—9:6 is, nevertheless, one of good news: the announcement of the birth of Hezekiah, that royal figure whose reign is marked by equity (9:1–6; compare 36:1—38:20 and 2 Kings 18:3–7).

Moreover, the "woe!" series is linked to another passage made up of strophes. The unit 9:7—10:4 consists of four parallel, small units which describe the apostasy of the House of Jacob. Each strophe deals with a different aspect of disobedience and concludes with a refrain which affirms the Lord's continuing anger. That very refrain also appears at the end of the six "woe!" strophes in 5:8–25, thus linking it to the second segment (9:7—12:6). In sum, the web of literary connections underscores the notion that all of the Lord's people—the kingdoms of Israel as well as of Judah—pervert justice into injustice.

When preachers deal with any one of the "woe!" strophes, they keep in mind the passage in its entirety. Its theme is the notion that the rejection of the Lord's word and law leads to apostasy. The first two and the fifth strophes deal in detail with failure to observe specific commandments, while the other three speak more broadly of that reversal which is caused by failure to conform to the spirit which the Law of Moses manifests.

The castigation of persons who keep amassing real estate (8–10) is based on the law of the jubilee year (Lev 25:8–20), according to which fields and houses revert every forty-ninth year to their original owners or, better, stakeholders in the Lord's land (see especially Lev 25:23). The story of King Ahab's foiled attempt to acquire Naboth's vineyard (not to mention the deceit and the murder which allowed him to do what he wanted) as well as the subsequent ruin of his royal house (1 Kings 21) illustrate the point.

The second and fifth strophes (11–17, 22–23) threaten with exile and destruction those whose drunkenness prevents them from perceiving the Lord at work. The elite's nonobservance of divinely set norms may express itself, as here, in the indiscriminate use of intoxicants. Does not the law stipulate that priests on duty abstain from alcohol so as to be able to give instruction (Lev 10:8–10)? Another passage spells out in graphic detail the irresponsible behavior of drunk priests and prophets (28:7–13).

The next three strophes address the disobedient in more general terms. First, there are persons who make themselves guilty by demanding a quick fulfillment of divine plans, before the time of their fruition (18–19). They fail to grasp that the Lord's counsel is one of long-range goals, spanning generations—does not the parable of the farmer (28:23–29) explain that timely actions, each in its proper season, mark the farmer's as well as the Lord's work?

Secondly, there are persons whose actions pervert what they touch: good into evil, light into dark, sweet into bitter (20). The repeated demands of Deuteronomy to eliminate "the evil from your midst" (Deut 13:16; 21:22) refer to actions contrary to the Lord's law and illustrate the point. By the same token, passages illustrating that darkness and bitterness come over those who are not obedient (Amos 5:18–20; Exod 15:22–26) indicate in what manner these notions are understood. Thirdly, there are people who are proud of their own powers of discernment (21), contrary to the notion that the Lord is the source of insight and wisdom (Jer 9:22–23; Gen 41:39; Prov 26:12).

The conclusion of the passage (26–30) describes in painfully vivid images the fate of the disloyal. They must endure the irresistible advance of powerful armies who, like animals of prey, claim their spoil. The miseries brought by foreign soldiers (be they Egyptian or Assyrian), experienced more than once by the people of Israel and Judah, are the Lord's chastisement, temporary though it may be (26:20–21; 54:4–10).

Isaiah's Vision of His Mandate (6:1–13)

"Holy! Holy! Holy!" The seraphim's call echoes around the globe through the centuries. The singing of the "Trishagion" is a central act of adoration and celebration in the liturgies of almost all churches.

The sixth chapter of Isaiah is the origin of the chant. There the prophet's vision is described as the setting of a double exchange: that between the celestial beings and Isaiah and, following it, that between the Lord and the prophet. The spoken words are terse and the contrasts of "pure" and "impure," of divine command and prophetic query, sharply formulated, giving the passage a tone of starkness and finality.

The prophet's vision translates him to the innermost part of the Temple in Jerusalem, into "the Holy of Holies." There he is allowed to glimpse the divine presence, enthroned, clothed in splendor, and surrounded by heavenly beings whose call Isaiah hears—a call claiming the whole world as the Lord's domain (1–4). Isaiah, realizing that he has seen that which a human being may not see and live, laments his certain death. But he is granted life through an act of purification, performed by one of the celestial creatures with a burning coal from the altar in front of the Temple (5–7).

With that admission to the heavenly court the vision turns into a divine-prophetic dialogue: in response to his offer to become the Lord's messenger, Isaiah is commissioned to delay Israel's comprehension of the divine plan until, generations later, they have endured not one but two devastations of their land and two exiles of their elite to foreign regions (8–13).

The preacher notes the text's wide horizons in time and space. Thus, while all the inhabited world—notably Assyria and Babylonia, Egypt and Cush—is in the sovereign power of Israel's God (compare 18:1–7; 19:24–25; 40:21–24), the Lord is worshiped by pilgrims from "far and near" in the Temple of the holy city (33:13–16; 49:14–21; 60:1–22). By the same token, the prophet envisions the coming and going of Israel's opponents during the span of almost two centuries: first the Assyrians in two waves devastating the Kingdom of Israel, laying low its ten tribes and exiling its leading people to northern Mesopotamia, then some four generations later the Babylonians, who in (at least) two campaigns make an end of the Kingdom of Judah, exiling the two remaining tribes of Benjamin and Judah.

However, the survivors of these disasters are compared to the shoots which the stump of a felled tree sends forth. Remnants do remain, are eventually freed from their divinely imposed blindness, and are granted the insight denied their forebears of Isaiah's time (13b; compare 1:9; 14:1–2; 44:24–28). Is not the opening of closed minds the mission of the divinely sent messengers in Isaiah's train—then as well as now (compare 42:18–25; 50:10–11; 61:1–3)?

Sermons may highlight the manner in which the message of the entire book is condensed into the prophet's mandate: the thematic movement from the ruin of the Lord's vineyard

(5:1–7) to its replanting as a veritable Garden of Eden (27:2–9; 51:1–3; 65:15–25). Preaching may also deal with the notion of the holiness of Israel's God, manifest in the inscrutability of divine counsel, the Lord's incomparability to other divine beings, and the sovereign power of Israel's God (40:12–26; compare Deut 4:1–39). Finally, the prophet's sense of the divine presence as well as his readiness to accept a heartrending mandate may become a sermon starter: "Isaiah in the footsteps of Moses" (compare Exod 3:1—4:17).

The Immanuel Sign (7:1—8:10)

"Behold, the young woman (the virgin, so the Greek Bible and KJV) will conceive and bear a son; but you shall name him 'With us is God'" (7:14). A familiar word—in Hebrew "immanu-el"—provides the guideword for the text and accordingly recurs at its end (8:8, 10).

In fact, the passage introduces two children to be born and symbolically named. One is the son of the king, the other of the prophet (7:10–17; 8:1–4). Both names are portents of the hardening of heart of which the preceding text speaks. Yet these signs and signals are understood only by those who have been given eyes to see. Thus Isaiah recognizes them while the people do not. The prophet may even make their meanings known, but his contemporaries persist in opposition (compare 8:11–12).

The prophetic encouragement of King Ahaz, who is afraid of the Aramean-Ephraimite siege (7:1–9), is the setting for two divine discourses: one reproaches Ahaz for his failure to accept the offer of a sign and then speaks of future, still greater devastations by the Assyrians (7:10–17, 18–25); the other reassures Isaiah with the sign of the birth of a son and then affirms that all human counsels designed to harm Israel will eventually fail (8:1–4, 5–10).

But now also a rift between Israel and Isaiah appears. Hence the two following passages speak of the Lord's command to Isaiah to separate himself from the people (8:11–23) and of the birth of (the future King) Hezekiah, whose return to the Law of Moses will be harbinger of future blessing (9:1–6; compare Deut 28:1–14).

The Unbelief of a King (7:1–17)

King Ahaz' failure to be loyal to the Lord is illustrated in different ways in 2 Kings 16 and Isa 7. The two passages deal with the topic from varying perspectives: 2 Kings 16 speaks of Ahaz' replacement of the bronze altar, made and placed to face the Temple in accord with Moses' order. The king put another altar in its place, one he had constructed in imitation of one he had seen in Damascus. Thus he put aside what Moses had commanded (see Exod 40:29).

The text in Isaiah, however, castigates the monarch for his lack of faith in the Lord's power to intervene on behalf of Judah and Jerusalem when Aram and Ephraim attempted to draw him into their anti-Assyrian alliance and, failing to do so, threatened to make an end of the Davidic dynasty. In other words, 2 Kings addresses Ahaz' ritual transgression, Isa 7 his lack of faith.

The king's failure to believe is made plain in an encounter between him and the prophet at an installation important for the city's water supply, expecially when a siege threatens: "at the intake of the conduit of the Upper Pool, at the Fullers' Field road"—the very place where a generation later King Hezekiah has his officers meet the Assyrian officers and respond in a manner which does prove that king's faith in the Lord (36:1—37:1)! Moreover, the threatened demise of the Davidic royal house is contrasted with the divine gift of a sign which signals its continuance, the announcement of the birth of the future King Hezekiah: he will be conceived by "the young woman," presumably the queen of twenty-year-old Ahaz (the Greek Bible [Septuagint] and older Christian versions such as KJV here employ the word "virgin," possibly referring to King Ahaz' still virginal queen-to-be).

A sermon may focus on the theme "faith" as the mainstay of those who are loyal to the Lord. The motif is couched in 9b as a pun. It employs the wordroot "amen" (reliable, trusty, firm, well-founded, sure) and does so in two ways: "If you do not make yourself firm (in the Lord), you will not be affirmed (by the Lord)." The word and its linguistic root are familiar from the concluding affirmation of prayers and solemn statements common in the Bible, the Synagogue, and the Church.

In the context of the Scriptures it calls to mind not only the "other" name which Israel's God is given in Isa 65:15-16— "The God of Amen"—but also the identification of the risen Jesus as "the Amen, the faithful and true witness, the beginning of God's creation" (Rev 3:14).

On the other hand, the preacher may wish to deal with the divine gift of signs—a familiar notion in the Hebrew Scriptures and in the NT as well (see Deut 4:34-35 and Luke 2:12). In Isa 7:10-17 the name of the child to be born is the sign. How? That very child, King Hezekiah, reversed his predecessor's defiance of the Law of Moses by reforming certain features of the cult in the Temple (compare 2 Kings 16:10-18 with 2 Kings 18:3-6 and 2 Chron 29:1—31:21). Do not the events of that king's reign demonstrate that the Lord was indeed the protector of the kingdom and of its monarch, rescuing them from certain perdition at the hand of the Assyrians (2 Kings 18:13—20:11 - Isa 36:1—38:20)?

Finally, a preacher may wish to explore a related, broader theme, that of the birth of not only this one savior-to-be but other deliverers. Does not 11:1-16 celebrate the future birth of King Josiah, a deliverer a century after Hezekiah? That ruler continued in Hezekiah's footsteps, bringing a peaceable kingdom to the sacred mountain, albeit for only a brief period. By the same token does not Matt 1:18-25 look toward the birth of Jesus of Nazareth from Mary, doing so in the spirit and drawing on the words of Isa 7?

Instruments of Divine Castigation (7:18-25)

The result of the king's unbelief is described in four vignettes, each different and striking in its imagery. The spread of enemy troops throughout the land is compared to that of Nile flies (Exod 8:16-27) and of Mesopotamian bees, and their pillaging to a razor's shaving all hair off the body (7:18-19, 20). The subsequent relinquishment of field and vineyard gives free reign to thorns and thistles (7:21-22, 23-25).

Preachers are familiar with the biblical notion that powerful kings and their imposing armies are but instruments in the hand of the God of Israel. Thus Assyria is "the rod of the Lord's anger" which, when it transgresses the set limits, is itself threatened with annihilation (10:5-19; compare 10:24-

32; 14:24–27). Aram and Ephraim on the one hand and Babylonia on the other are similarly "staffs" of divine intervention (7:4–7; 14:12–22; 47:8–11). The actions of these world powers attest nothing but the sovereignty of the Lord.

The Vindication of Immanu-El (8:1–10)

The passage is full of notable images, bold assertions, and resolute actors: a tablet inscribed with a symbolic name and the birth of a son to the prophet, the gentle flow of a brook and the raging waters of a river in flood, and the assurance of divine protection signified by still another symbolic name. In visionary-meditative style the prophet moves from narrative (1–4) to quotation of divine words (5–8) and then to triumphant shout (9–10). Also, the last two small units are connected by rhyme: both end with the symbolic name given to the royal child to be born (7:10–17), though in the first instance the prince is addressed by name, while in the second his name's translated meaning "God is with us" clinches the prophet's affirmation of the Lord's protection of Judah and Jerusalem.

The passage interprets the political events of the last third of the eighth century B.C.E. as planned and carried out by Israel's God. There is the failure of the anti-Assyrian alliance of King Rezin of Damascus and King Pekah of Samaria—a pact into which King Ahaz of Jerusalem did not let himself be drawn (734/3 B.C.E.; compare 7:1–9). There is the despoiling and exiling of the northern portion of the Kingdom of Israel by the Assyrians in response to that alliance (8:1–4; compare 2 Kings 15:29). Finally, there is the complete demise, some ten years later, of the Northern Kingdom (722 B.C.E.; 8:5–8; compare 2 Kings 17:1–6). Fittingly, the passage concludes with the assurance of divine protection (8:9–10), symbolized by the name of the already conceived, but as yet unborn, royal child.

Preaching on the text may deal with the power of the religious symbol: a monarch's and a prophet's child are both given metaphoric names. These are signs for those able to perceive their significance. The name of Isaiah's child refers to the immediate future and relates to the opponents' defeat;

that of the royal child points to events in the more distant future and to the eventual deliverance of the faithful remnant. In both instances a high degree of reflection has generated terse passages dense in meaning.

The Mandate of Isaiah's Disciples (8:11–23a)

The rift has now widened. The prophet finds himself opposed to his king, and Isaiah's followers are told to withdraw from their contemporaries. The text begins with the prophet's quoting the Lord's order that Isaiah oppose the people's fear of the Aramean-Ephraimite alliance. The divine word demands that he reject his people's dread, that he fear only the Lord, and finally that he "seal testimony and instruction" within the disciples (11–16).

Isaiah responds with the affirmation that he will continue to hope for his people's eventual obedience; he and his followers (literally: male children) will persist as "signs and portents" in Israel, set up by the Lord (17–18). Finally, the disciples are instructed to reproach the people for their consultation of "soothsayers and diviners," to call them back to Isaiah's "instruction and testimony" (note the inversion of the two words in the phrase) which are now preserved within them, and to announce despair to those who continue to turn away (19–23a).

The preacher notes that the divine mandate is foreshadowed in the passage describing Isaiah's visionary reception of his own mandate—a mandate which sets him over against a hardened people (6:1–13). It is taken up in later texts which speak of the continued presence of the Lord's word and spirit in Israel through the mediation of Isaiah's successors (59:21; compare 48:16b; 50:4–9; 54:11–17). Thus the prophetic witness to the Law of Moses and to its promises of life, not death, for the obedient remains an invitation to those who have ears to hear. The traditions of Israel—and then of Synagogue and Church—know of periodic rediscoveries of that ancient offer of blessing. King Josiah's obedience to the unexpectedly recovered lawbook is one example (11:1–9; compare 2 Kings 22:1—23:25 and 2 Chron 34:1—35:19). Later instances are early Christian affirmations of the Law of Moses (for example,

Matt 5:17–48) or the call heard time and again in Jewish writings to honor and to preserve that Law (for example, Pirqe Aboth 1).

A homily may explore the notion of the concealment of the divine presence from those who refuse to respond to its summons—not to mention the cry of many faithful servants that the presence of the Lord has become inaccessible to them, too! Periods of misery and despair (21–23a) are endured even by those whose faithfulness is unquestioned. They are counseled to take comfort in the assurance that the experience of divine absence, even of the Lord's anger, will not last for ever but will subside as "the waters of Noah" did (54:4–10; compare 26:20–21). The prophet's own waiting for a God who hides (17) is indeed a portent of the reversal certain to come, when "the knowledge of the Lord will fill the land like waters cover the sea" (11:9).

The Celebration of the King of Peace (8:23b—9:6)

Exuberant in word and thought, the text envisions the sudden end of Assyrian domination and celebrates the birth of a king as its cause. He is that ruler whose symbolic name "God is with us" has already been announced (7:10–17; compare 8:5–10) and during whose reign Jerusalem will be miraculously rescued from the siege which the army from Nineveh lays against it (36:1—37:38). From contempt to honor, from violence to peace, from darkness to light—these are the transitions which dominate the passage.

Hezekiah is the prince who is given the four well-known titles of honor or throne names (9:5). The political events of the last third of the eighth century B.C.E., as told in 2 Kings 15:8—20:21 (and 2 Chron 27:1—32:33), provide background and commentary: after the reign of King Ahaz, that of Hezekiah was also doubly threatened. From without the Assyrian power continued to overshadow Syria-Palestine, and from within apostasy remained a temptation. Nevertheless, the king is praised because his rule measured up to the standard set by David (see 2 Kings 18:3; 22:2 and compare 2 Sam 8:15).

Sermons may deal with the manner in which words of assurance and celebration bring to climax and conclusion a sustained text segment (5:1—9:6). It begins with reproaches and the announcement of the people's divinely ordered blindness. The following segment (9:7—12:6) similarly leads its audience from chastisement to hope, from Israel's apostasy to the birth of Josiah, another king after the Lord's heart (11:1–9).

Homilies may also explore the four throne names given to the king (9:5). The notion of the good king's "wise counsel" is in accord with the Lord's removal and eventual reinstitution of counselors "as in the beginning" (1:26; compare 3:3). On the other hand, his "mighty strength" is demonstrated by his faith under adverse conditions (37:1; 38:9–20); his "eternal fatherhood" to the royal house (and hence to the nation) makes him the standard for generations to come. Most of all, as "prince of peace" he brings and makes manifest that well-being and blessing which the Law of Moses holds out to the observant (see Deut 28:1–14 as well as Lev 26:3–13 and Num 6:24–26). Little wonder that texts which celebrate the coming of a deliverer employ themes and words derived from this passage (compare 11:1–9 and Eph 2:14).

Isaiah's Vision of the Lord's Peace (9:7—12:6)

The prophet's mandate within the Lord's vineyard is spelled out in the preceding segment (5:1—9:6): from the year of King Uzziah's death onward he and his disciples are "signs and portents," set up by their divine master among the people of the vineyard (8:17–18). The second segment (9:7—12:6) will now lay out what the prophetic eye sees for the coming century: Jacob-Israel's divinely sanctioned downfall (9:7—10:4), but also Assyria's failure to subdue Jerusalem (10:5–34), and then, generations later, the appearance of Josiah, Jesse's shoot, who unites and pacifies those alienated from each other (11:1–10) and calls home those who have been exiled, inspiring the returnees to a new song, a song of deliverance (11:11–16; 12:1–6).

Jacob-Israel—Target of the Lord's Anger (9:7—10:4)

The Lord's "outstretched" arm is the symbol of sovereign, divine power; do not the stories of Israel's rescue from Egypt time and again speak of the divine intervention "with outstretched arm" (Exod 6:6; Deut 26:8)? The phrase "outstretched" occurs no fewer than four times in the refrains which end the strophes detailing the Lord's continuing anger (9:7–11; 12–16, 17–20; 10:1–4)! But now, many centuries after the Exodus from the land of the Nile, the divine intervention is directed not to Israel's adversaries but to Israel itself. The divine action this time has inflicted plight and disaster on the Lord's own people (compare Jer 21:1–7).

The strophes, building up to a climax, are connected to what precedes and to what follows: the lament call "O for . . . ," which begins the last strophe, is repeated at the opening of the next passage (10:5–34); it is also the lament call which appears six times in 5:8–30, the passage at the beginning of the first segment 5:1—9:6. There is a further literary connection between the two segments: the fourfold refrain of 9:7—10:4 appears also at the end of that earlier strophe series (5:25b). In short, great care is taken to align the predicaments of Judah and Israel; both alike are the targets of the Lord's indignation.

Sermons may explore these forward- and backward-looking connections. Not only do Israel and Judah equally fail in their loyalty to their divine master (promising though their beginnings had been, see 5:7), but also Assyria, the seemingly successful agent of the divine plan, is brought low, and that for the same reason that Israel and Judah are defeated—arrogance (compare 10:13–14 with 9:8). Indeed, what ancient Greek writers castigated as vainglory or *hybris* is in Isaiah condemned as the root cause of public folly, both among the Lord's own people and among the nations, the descendants of Abraham and Noah (see also 14:13–14). By the same token, the divinely sanctioned chastisement of Israel is followed in due time and in response to the people's return to the Lord, by the promise of healing and new life (see 26:20–21; 54:4–10; also 1 Peter 4:17).

On the other hand, a homily may deal with the manner in which the divine calls to obedience become increasingly insistent and the descriptions of the people's misery more and more sinister. First, boasts of rebuilding fallen-down houses in grander style are countered by enemy threats from East and West (9:9-11; compare 2 Kings 16:7-9), then the failure to recognize the divine at work is made manifest in the ruin "in one day" of those holding high offices (9:12-16; compare 2 Kings 17:1-6). Finally, the observation is made that strife between siblings leads to internecine warfare (9:17-20; compare 2 Kings 16:5). Contempt for the Law of Moses is shown to be the harbinger of the utter destruction which indeed befell the Kingdom of Israel (10:1-4; compare 10:2 [and 1:17] with Deut 16:16-18 and 10:18).

The notion of the certain fulfillment of the Lord's word may be made the basis of a sermon. The passage begins with the pointed reference to that word which "the Lord sent among the people of Jacob so that it came to rest (literally: to fall) in Israel"—possibly a reference to the preaching of Amos and Hosea (compare Hos 6:4-11; Amos 5:1-3). Do not the grim events of the last twenty-five years of the existence of the Northern Kingdom (746-722 B.C.E.; see 2 Kings 15:8—17:41) demonstrate the fulfillment of what the divine word had announced? Does it not accomplish its purpose without fail, like the rain which descends from the sky to water the earth and to bring forth fruit (55:10-11)?

Assyria—Rod of the Lord's Anger (10:5-32)

The kings of Nineveh were for the Kingdom of Judah a far greater threat then was the Israelite-Aramean alliance. While Isa 9:7—10:4 announces the demise of the monarchy in Samaria, the following passage 10:5-34 turns to the future fate of Assyria. It reviews first in two somewhat parallel paragraphs (5-12, 13-19) the success-intoxicated arrogance of Assyrian rulers and sets against it the Lord's affirmation that pride does come before the fall. It then projects the coming reversal (20-34): the return of Israel's remnant (20-23), the safety of Zion's inhabitants (24-26), and (possibly) the way stations of the Assyrians' doomed march on Jerusalem (27-32).

The passage is cast in a reflective-visionary mold, hence it moves from lament to quotation and announcement, again to quotation, then to rhetorical question, and finally to announcements of future events. Also notable is the imagery of birds, their nests and eggs (14–15), and the use of the guidewords "light" and "fire" (16–17).

Castigation of Imperial Pride (10:5–19)

The horizon of the passage in time and space is comprehensive. No fewer than seven kingdoms and their actual or anticipated subjection to Assyrian rulers are mentioned. The list begins with Carcemish, the city farthest from Jerusalem (located on the banks of the upper Euphrates), and ends with the emperor's boast that Jerusalem will surely share the fate of the six cities already conquered. On the other hand, the prophet's speech spans the reigns of four kings: Tiglathpileser III, who captured Calno, Arpad, and Damascus; then Salmaneser V, who began the siege of Samaria; and Sargon II, who took it as well as Hamath and Carcemish. The survey ends with Sennacherib's attempted capture of Jerusalem in 701 B.C.E.; the announcement of the Lord's rescue of Zion from that attack is the climax of this passage and of the following one (compare 12 with 27 and 33–34).

The text emphasizes the Lord's sovereignty in the face of the Assyrian kings' claims to absolute power. Their armies are highly disciplined and well equipped (5:26–29) and their commanders very competent, having subdued all of Syria-Palestine, deposing kings who resisted and making vassals of those who submitted (8–9; compare 2 Kings 17:1–6). Nevertheless, Sennacherib did fail in his bid to capture Jerusalem and must be told that his boasting is of no avail: Does the axe vaunt itself against the person who wields it? The Assyrian ruler's unsuccessful attempt to take Judah's capital (10:11) is narrated in detail in 36:1—37:38, which thus offers background information as well as commentary on 10:5–19.

A sermon may explore the prophetic claim that Zion's God is not powerless, as are the other deities who could not protect their cities. Through miraculous intervention (10:12, 17; 37:7, 21–35, 36) the Lord proves to be more powerful than they (14:24–27; 40:12–26). Those who several generations later despair over Jerusalem's capture and destruction by the Babylonians must thus be reminded that not once but twice in the past a divine rescue of David's royal city was prophetically announced beforehand and then actually occurred. Is this not reason to expect that now also, after the Babylonians' capture of Jerusalem, the Lord's earlier announcement of their eventual defeat will come true (compare 48:1–11)? In short, faith in the Lord sees the God of Israel at work through the lead figures of world events and recognizes that whether they themselves know it or not, the Lord acts through them on behalf of his "servant Jacob" and of "Israel, his beloved " (45:3–7; compare also Rom 8:28–30).

Announcements of Coming Reversals (10:20–32)

A remnant's return, a city's restored confidence, and an imperial army foiled; these are the memorable surprises of Hezekiah's reign. The prophet pegs them to "that day" (20, 27), the occasion of the Lord's deliverance of Jerusalem from the Assyrian encirclement in 701 B.C.E. (36:1—37:38-2 Kings 18:13—19:37). However, the text inverts the order of the events and speaks first of the results of that rescue (20–23, 24–26) and only then of the doomed attack, more exactly of some thirteen way stations (at least so it seems) of the enemy army in its advance from the North to Nob, a town overlooking the holy city (27, 28–32).

A sermon may deal with the manner in which the coming reversal is described. Striking images appear in preceding passages in Isaiah and "A Book of Remembrance" (Genesis–Malachi, as ordered in the Hebrew Bible; see the Introduction for the relation between Isaiah and that larger literary work of which it is conceptually a part). Thus, "A Remnant Will Return," the symbolic name of Isaiah's son, is transformed into an affirmation of Jacob's return. It refers to the practice of people left in the territory of the former Kingdom of Israel who would make pilgrimages to Jerusalem (compare 21 with 7:2 and Jer 41:4–5). By the same token, that return is directed to the "Mighty Hero," a reference to Hezekiah, the very royal figure whose birth has already been announced (compare 21 with 9:5). Indeed, according to another writing contained in the Hebrew Scriptures, it was King Hezekiah who invited those who had remained loyal to the Law of Moses and were left as remnants in the tribal areas of Ephraim, Manasseh, Asher, and Zebulon to observe the Passover by coming to Mount Zion for its observance (2 Chron 30:10–13). Was not Hezekiah a ruler who was loyal to the Lord in an exemplary manner (2 Kings 18:3–7)? The removal of the Assyrian yoke, announced in 9:3, is also celebrated in this passage (27) with nearly identical words. Finally, stories of deliverance from the threats posed first by the Egyptians and later the Midianites supply images for the description of the rescue from Nineveh (compare 24 and 26 with 9:3 and with Judg 7:1—8:21 and Exod 14:15–31).

The use of the "scriptural" pictures presents the salvation from the threats of mighty kings of a new time as but the newest entry in the already well-established list of divine interventions on Israel's behalf. Such additions to "the loyal acts of the Lord" (Ps 103:6) also inspire texts which follow, for example, 11:10–16; 43:16–21; 48:20–21. In fact, many writings in early Christianity and Judaism are molded by the same sense of continuity with the deliverances of old (see Pirqe Aboth 1:1 [Mishnah] and Acts 7:2–53 [NT]).

Jesse's Shoot—Standard of Justice (10:33—11:10)

Metaphors abound: the downfall of lofty trees of Lebanon, the appearance of a tender shoot, the girdle of justice, even a lion eating straw, indications that the prophet perceives what can only be expressed figuratively and thus remains, as it were, behind a veil.

After Assyria's withdrawal from Judah and Jerusalem (10:33–34), a ruler who is, like David, descended from Jesse will arise (11:1). His reign will introduce an altogether new standard of justice (11:2–5) and enable those who are opposed to each other to change their ways and live in peace, once gathered on the Lord's holy hill (11:6–9). Moreover, the descendants of Noah and Abraham, dispersed through the inhabited world, will recognize that king as a sign which bids them come to Zion and there seek the Lord's guidance (11:10). The king praised in this singular manner is Josiah (640–609 B.C.E.). Hence the passage celebrates his prompt, obedient response to "the lawbook" discovered in the Temple when repairs were carried out at his order (2 Kings 22:1—23:30, esp. 22:2 and 23:25).

This insight opens the text for preachers and commentators. The king's "knowledge and fear of the Lord" (11:2) refers to his promulgation and observance of "the lawbook" (= Deut 5:1—30:20, according to Deut 1:5 the summary rehearsal of Exodus—Numbers by Moses before his death). Does it not direct the king to acquire his own copy of that law for personal study and guidance (Deut 17:14–20)? Does it not move the adjudication of law cases which cannot be decided in the (lower) local courts to the (higher) officers in Jerusalem (Deut 17:8–13)? Does it not generally oblige all Israelites, especially judges and administrators, to see to it that "justice" is done, that is, to enforce the regulations which the Law of Moses (rather than other law codes) enjoins (Deut 16:18–20)? Does it not specifically forbid one "to look at someone's face" (be partial), when a trial is under way (compare 11:3b with Deut 16:19)? Or does it not demand "just treatment" of the lowly, as indeed the Law of Moses requires (compare 11:4 with Lev 19:15)? Finally, does it not stipulate that "two or three witnesses" be heard in capital cases, forestalling judgments based on what only one pair of eyes or ears have seen and heard, and thus avoiding spilling innocent blood (Deut 17:2–7)? In short, the portrayal of the just king in 11:1–10 is drawn with the lines and colors of Deuteronomy.

Once the innocent and the guilty are identified according to these "just" standards, which are admired worldwide as "fair" and are perceived as evidence of Israel's "wisdom" (Deut 4:5–8), the king who promulgates and enforces them may be said to wear "justice as a girdle" (compare 11:5 with Deut 16:20). Tribal groups who may have different legal standards now find themselves unified under the one Law of Moses as kept and administered in Jerusalem.

In light of this observation it is possible that the listing of no fewer than thirteen animals, some of whom are deadly enemies but who encounter each other peacefully on Mount Zion, metaphorically describes the intertribal harmony the Law of Moses creates. After all, the figurative description of tribes as animals is illustrated by the Blessing of Jacob (Gen 49:1–27) and the Blessing of Moses (Deut 33:1–29). There different tribes are compared to lion, ass, serpent, hind, wolf, and ox.

By the same token, the mention of "a boy who will lead

them" may refer to King Josiah, who began his reign when he was eight years old (compare 11:6b with 2 Kings 22:1 and 2 Chron 34:3). Josiah's introduction of the Law of Moses as ultimate guide in legal and cultic matters makes Jerusalem once for all the center for the law-observing descendants of Jacob, who regularly appear before the Lord in Jerusalem, celebrating the festivals and encountering each other on "the Lord's holy hill." The preacher may explore the promises of well-being, blessing, and peace as they are set forth in the Law of Moses, especially Deut 28:1–14, and as they are realized through persons singularly loyal to that divine instruction, whether Josiah, Hezekiah, or the many others who lay claim to that distinction before and after them. A homily may focus on this imagery which is creative as well as scriptural, announcing to the faithful a peaceful existence in a veritable Garden of Eden (compare 51:3; Deut 11:21 and 33:28; also Rom 15:7–12).

Jesse's Root—Ensign for Ingathering (11:11—12:6)

The notion of a second exodus! Nothing less than a repetition of Israel's archetypal deliverance from Egypt is envisioned. King Josiah's promulgation of the Law of Moses as the only standard of justice for the dispersed descendants of Jacob, and the king's elevation of Jerusalem as their one sacral and judicial center, are invitations to all who are willing to listen. They now can carry out what Josiah's reform has made possible. They are invited to make pilgrimages to the holy city to celebrate Israel's inherited feasts there and to have difficult cases settled by the judge in office in Jerusalem.

Moreover, the Assyrian imperial power, which had held Syria-Palestine in its iron grip during several generations before Josiah, was waning. In fact, Nineveh fell in 612 B.C.E. The change in world affairs gave subdued and exiled peoples a new lease on life. Little wonder that Josiah made the most of the situation and sought to restore David's empire, welcoming the displaced, especially the elite of the ten (northern) tribes who had been taken captive to Assyria (11:11; compare 2 Kings 15:29; 17:6) or who had sought refuge in Egypt (compare 1 Kings 11:40; 2 Kings 23:34; also Jer 43:1–7). The prophet-visionary fittingly concludes this segment with a description of the coming days of new freedom and with the songs of deliverance which the redeemed will sing (12:1–6).

The preacher may explore the symbols of holy city and sacral feast, both of which remain central for Jews and Christians as tangible tokens of the divine presence (compare 33:17–24 and Luke 2:41–51). The identification of religious centers gives to individual and corporate life seasons of celebration and places of devotion. Does the psalmist not rejoice when the call is heard, "Let us go unto the House of the Lord" (Ps 122:1)?

A sermon may also deal with the manner in which the second and greater exodus (11:11—12:6) is described in the verbal imagery of the first. Not only is the parallel between the second and the first expressly set forth (11:16), but also related aspects of the escape from oppression are highlighted: the strength of the divine hand (11:11; compare Exod 14:16), the crossing of water as one traverses dry land (11:15; compare Exod 14:22), and songs of deliverance couched in hallowed words (12:2b; compare Exod 15:2a). On the other hand, the ways in which the second exodus transcends the first may be detailed as well: now the Lord gathers the dispersed not merely from one place but "from the four corners of the earth" (11:12), now estranged siblings become reconciled (11:13; compare 11:1–9) and live unmolested in harmony (11:14; compare 9:9–11). In sum, 12:1–6 celebrates what Moses' song of deliverance anticipates, the Lord's exaltation on his holy mountain: "Thou wilt bring them in, and plant them on thy own mountain, the place, O Lord, which thou hast made for thy abode, the sanctuary, O Lord, which thy hands have established. The Lord will reign for ever and ever" (Exod 15:17–18).

The Invitation to the Chastised Nations (13:1—27:13)

The second section of the first part of the book conforms to the thematic structure which is characteristic of Isa 1—66. It leads the audience from chastisement to consolation, from reproach to promise. The comprehensive description of the rout of the nations (13—23) introduces a similarly wide-ranging portrayal of the Lord's reversal of Israel's and the nations' humiliation (24—27), climaxing in the announcement that on festive Mount Zion tears, shame, and even death shall be overcome for those who have followed the invitation to the banquet of the Lord (25:6–8).

The Rout of the Nations (13:1—23:18)

The divine scourging of no fewer than twelve nations is described in these texts, sometimes in extensive poems (13:2—14:23; 15:1—16:14), sometimes in brief, even cryptic sayings (14:28–32; 21:11–12). At times the rescue of Israel or even of some of the other nations is announced; at times the prophet's agony over the fall of a neighbor of Israel is eloquently described (14:1–2, 32; 16:5; 23:15–18; also 15:5). The worldwide upheaval, described in the following segment 24—27, is anticipated within the universal perspective of 19:24–25 or 21:9–10. It is balanced, as it were, by the emphasis on Mount Zion as the central place of refuge where "the humble of the Lord find shelter" (14:32; compare 16:5; 17:7–8; 18:7).

Most of the units relating to a particular nation are titled "Burden concerning . . ."—a title which means something like "summary word concerning (a nation's fate and future)." The sustained series is designed to illustrate fully what some verses within the segment state summarily. Thus 14:26 (compare 24:1 and 27:1) says that "this is the purpose which is purposed concerning the whole earth; and this is the hand that is stretched out over all the nations." The series corresponds to similar ones found in Jer 46—51, Ezek 25—32, and Amos 1:2—2:16. In all series the nations named are those whose opposition to the people of the Lord is attested in "A Book of Remembrance" (Genesis–Malachi, as ordered in the Hebrew Bible; see the discussion in the Introduction). It was among them that law-abiding descendants of Jacob-Israel, and also of Isaac and Rebecah, Abraham and Sarah, and Noah's three sons lived. At times they are identified by the names of their host nations (see Acts 2:9). However, as people living in dispersion they are invited, even urged, to make Zion their spiritual home, that is, to make the pilgrimage to the holy city and to celebrate feasts of the sacred year within its walls. Also those who live in Syria-Palestine, even in Jerusalem itself, are included in that invitation (17:1–11; 22:1–

14)—are they not equally called to the exclusive observance of Moses' law and to the worship on Mount Zion (49:1–6; compare Amos 2:2–5, 6–16)?

The Burden of Babylon (13:1—14:23)

This sustained composition describes the onslaught on Babylon by the Medes (and the Persians under King Cyrus in 539 B.C.E.) as "the day of the Lord" (13:2–22), announces a second election of Jacob-Israel by the Lord (14:1–2), quotes words of satisfaction over and ridicule of vain Babylon's end (14:3–21), and concludes with a double citation of the Lord's affirmation of the oppressor's complete destruction (14:22–23). Thus the unit alternates between complementary notions: that of earth-shaking collapse and that of reassuring restoration. It is identified as "burden," presumably best understood as comprehensive statement which "bears" all that is to be said and known in relation to the superpower. Moreover, Isaiah "saw" it, in keeping with the visionary mode of prophetic speaking, a mode not narrowly bound to time and space. After all, the prophet's perspective takes in two centuries as well as a forbidding stretch of North Arabian desert!

The Vision of Babylon's Fall and Israel's Return (13:2—14:2)

The ominous vision of the future of Nebuchadnezzar's capital moves swiftly: there is first the signal for the assembling of the siege troops ready to move against it (13:2–5), followed by the call to lament the city's anticipated destruction (13:6–8). Then there is the description of the upset of land and people, even of sun and moon, causing the few survivors to flee like frightened sheep (13:9–16). Then there is the divine announcement that it is the Lord who stirs up the Medes for the victorious attack, turning the metropolis into another Sodom, deserted by human beings and sought by hyenas (13:17–22). But Babylon's end is Israel's new beginning. Assured of divine favor, Israelites and Judaites return to their land, accompanied by proselytes and even served by their former masters (14:1–2).

The vivid imagery, striking as it is, alienates preachers called to witness to divine forgiveness and love. How dare one speak of women widowed or, worse, of infants dashed against rocks before their parents' eyes (13:16; compare Ps 137:9) as aspects of the Lord's action? Though Assyrian and Babylonian armies are known to have committed such acts, is it appropriate for a prophet of the Lord to attribute to Israel's God responsibility for such deeds, even if only done to those who had themselves committed them?

The answer is this: the visionary-reflective mode of prophetic speaking perceives all that occurs in time and space, be it "weal or woe," as divinely orchestrated, and that for the sake of Israel (45:1–8)! To be sure, when individuals and nations appointed to carry out the Lord's designs transgress the set limits, they are chastised and brought low. Do not the defeats of Assyria and Babylonia prove that very point (10:5–19; 14:13–15; 47:8–11)? Thus preachers are led to emphasize the Lord's all-causality as the overriding notion, asserting that the darkest aspects of human actions are not beyond the purview and control of the Lord. They also know that the last word of the God of Israel is a promise of blessing, well-being, peace, even freedom from sin and death, directed to those who are loyal to the Lord (19:24–25; 25:6–8; 66:18–20).

A sermon may focus on "the day of the Lord," a notion repeatedly discussed in "The Twelve Minor Prophets" (compare Isa 13:6, 9, 13 with Joel 1:15–18; Amos 5:18–20; Zeph 1:14–18; and Mal 3:23 [RSV: 4:5]). For mighty Babylon the day of the Lord is the moment of its downfall; on that day the fate appointed for it by the Lord fulfills itself (13:22b). Individuals and nations, no matter when in the course of time their "day" arrives, are exhorted to perceive in radical reversals the divine hand at work, to reflect on cause and effect, and to accept the challenge of new beginnings. For captive Israel (and Judah) this is the significance of Babylon's fall. Indeed, 14:1–2 promise a new election of Jacob-Israel, who will bring proselytes and their former masters with them when they (re-)turn to the land as settlers or pilgrims (compare 56:3–8; 58:1–14).

Preachers may also deal with the wide horizons opened by the text: across two centuries it envisions "a victorious one," divinely called "from a far land" (13:5) or "from the rising of the sun" (41:25), "a bird of prey from the East, the man of the Lord's counsel" (46:11). Here Cyrus, the Persian king who will set the captives free and allow Jerusalem and its Temple to be rebuilt, moves into the picture; in due place he will be honored with the titles "shepherd of the Lord" and "the anointed one" (44:28; 45:1). Thus the prophet can affirm that only Israel's God—and no one else among gods and human beings—announced of old what the future brings: Cyrus' victory over Babylon and his edict of release of the captive Judaites (compare 48:3, 5–7 with 13:17–18 and 21:1–10).

The Morning Star's Descent to the Underworld (14:3–23)

The poem introduces several actors, posts them at their stations, and has them speak their lines—a playwright at work! Once the Babylonian emperor, harsh ruler of the inhabited world, has been subdued, joy breaks forth on earth. Even the cedars on Mount Lebanon, no more felled by imperial building ambitions, rejoice (3–8).

The action then moves to another sphere, that of the underworld. There the deceased are present as shadows, continuing to hold the office and wear the insignia that identified them on earth. Their shadows stir in order to receive their Babylonian colleague. On earth he had far exceeded them in ambition, power, and splendor, but now he finds himself with them transferred to the place of maggots and worms and more humiliated than they (9–21). They rise to meet Nebuchadnezzar (his name is not given), confirm that he has arrived in the realm of decay, and liken his death to the fall of the morning star from the sky (9–11). They quote words of his heaven-storming arrogance, of his desire to place his throne above the stars on the mountain of the gods' assembly, and of his claim to nothing less than divine status (13–14). In bitter irony they observe that he has now arrived at the lowest place, causing all who witness the spectacle to comment in amazement on the reversal of his fortunes (15–21). Then, as from another realm, the Lord's voice breaks in, confirming the finality of Babylon's overthrow (22–23).

Readers and hearers are awed by the portrayal of this scene in Hades; it reminds them of another scene in "A Book of Remembrance"—that of desperate King Saul conjuring up through a diviner the shadow of Prophet Samuel, his erstwhile mentor (1 Sam 28). This encounter also spells doom and death: the spirit of Samuel can only confirm what he had announced to Saul before he departed to the realm of the dead.

Metaphoric and mythic images are woven into the passage: majestic trees who can speak, the comparison of the toppled king to "the son of the dawn" brought low, and references to the mountain of the gods whom ancient poets located "in the North." Finally, there is the quotation of the deposed ruler's claim to godlike status for himself—surely the highest arrogance imaginable. They serve to illustrate the proverb that "pride comes before the fall" (Prov 11:22). As a "parable concerning the King of Babylon" (4), the composition is a telling example of the manner in which the disobedient become "a proverb (literally: a parable) and a byword" (Deut 28:37; compare Rev 17:3b–6).

The Import of Assyria's Fate (14:24–27)

The quotation of the Lord's oath-confirmed announcement of Assyria's downfall (24–25) is followed by the prophetic assertion that its fate is the divine plan for all peoples (26–27). Here two emphases may be noted: the certainty of the fulfillment of the Lord's counsel, and the affirmation of the certain impact of what happens especially on the empire (of Assyria) whose capital is Nineveh. Either may be developed into a homily.

The announcement of the Assyrian empire's demise, already fully given in 10:5–32, is repeated after the (chronologically later) fall of Babylonia has been foretold (13:1—14:23). Thus that earlier theme is taken up again, anticipating the full narration of the overthrow of Assyria's power as it begins to take its course in Canaan (36:1—37:38). The triple repetition of the assertion of "the removal of the oppressor's yoke" (9:3a; 10:27 and 14:25b) alerts the audience to the importance of that notion.

A sermon may also explore the claim that a divine intervention directed against one adversary illustrates the pattern of further actions of the God of Israel in relation to all peoples. In fact, the series "Prophecies (or Burdens) concerning the Nations" (13:1—23:18) demonstrates the universal validity of this model of divine activity. Thus all nations are addressed and no people is exempted (14:26; compare Jer 25:15–38). By the same token, all are invited to become obedient to the divine will and to receive blessing and peace (2:2–4; 25:6–8; 45:20–23; compare Phil 2:5–11).

The Burden of Philistia (14:28–32)

Though subdued by King David two centuries earlier, the Philistines occasionally threatened the Kingdom of Judah. After the middle of the eighth century B.C.E. they, like other small nations of Syria-Palestine, found themselves overrun first by the Assyrians (20:1), later by the Egyptians (Jer 47:1–7), then by the Babylonians (Ezek 25:15–17), and finally by the Persians, not to mention outbreaks of violence between them and their immediate neighbors (Amos 1:6–8).

The vivid formulations of the passage must be seen in the light of this information. The joy of the Philistines over their release from Judaite supremacy (2 Chron 26:6) amounts, however, to self-deception because "the snake," having been warded off, begets a more dangerous one. The Assyrians, coming from the North like a fire, replace the King of Jerusalem as overlord, humiliate the coast dwellers, and as a result permit Judaites residing in Philistine lands to turn to Zion as pilgrims and worshipers (compare 2 Chron 28:18–19).

Preachers recognize in this brief text the comprehensive perspective of Isa 1—66. Though covering the period of only one generation, the vision illustrates the point made in the preceding passage: the powerful moves of emperors and their armies are but manifestations of the Lord's plan (compare 40:12–26).

The Burden of Moab (15:1—16:14)

Prophetic compassion does not end at Israel's borders! Isaiah raises his voice in lament for Moab (15:5; 16:9, 11); its ruin troubles him as deeply as that of Jerusalem and Judah. Refugees from Moab are invited to find shelter in Zion (16:1–5), but also the afflicted nation is promised the survival of a remnant, however small (16:13–14). The assurances are introduced by laments, the first of which concerns Moab's devastated cities (16:6–12). As elsewhere in Isaiah, the texts are paired and move from castigation to promise (see the discussion of the book's thematic structure in the Introduction). The two laments (15:1b–9 and 16:6–12) are each followed by words of hope: the first is an invitation to refugees (16:1–5) and the second a consolation for Moab (16:13–14).

Preachers note other prophecies concerning Moab in "The Latter Prophets": Jer 48:1–47, Ezek 25:8–11, Amos 2:1–2, and Zeph 2:8–11—these also conform to the compositional principles observable in their books. For instance, the prophecy in Jeremiah ends, like several other prophecies in Jer 46—51, with the promise of restoration (48:37; compare 26:28; 49:7, 39), and the castigation of Moab in Amos 2:1–2 fits into the pattern of Amos 1:2—2:16. Thus each book's series of prophecies concerning neighboring nations interprets their fate and future within the context of that book. On the other hand, the word-for-word correspondence of Isa 15:2–7 with Jer 48:37, 38, 5, 36 and of Isa 16:6–10 with Jer 48:29–33 stresses the continuing validity of Isaiah's words directed to Moab—does not Jeremiah, one of Isaiah's successors, repeat them?

The Call to Moab's Refugees (15:1b—16:5)

No fewer than seventeen place names appear in the call to mourning in 15:1b–9—a veritable lesson in Moabite geography! Similar extensive listings are found elsewhere in Isaiah, such as that of the thirteen way stations of the Assyrian army advancing against Jerusalem (10:28–32) or that of the twenty-one items of feminine adornment which will be taken away from Judah's leading women (3:18–23), but also the (much shorter) list of Egypt, Assyria, and Israel as the three "peoples of the Lord" (19:24–25), not to mention the listing of the six nations who are invited to come (on five different means of conveyance!) to worship in Jerusalem (66:18–20).

The appearance of such catalogues illustrates the comprehensive worldview of the visionary-prophet—a perspective which seeks to include many nations and periods and to relate them to the center of the prophet's world: the holy city on Mount Zion within the worldwide community of Israel (16:5; compare 14:1–2, 32; 18:7; 19:23; 25:6–8; and 35:8–10).

A sermon may deal with the emphasis on justice and righteousness which those coming to "the Tent of David" will find in Zion. King Josiah's (anticipated) promulgation of the Law of Moses as the only standard of justice in Israel makes the king and judge in Jerusalem the final arbiter for all cases (compare 2:2–4 and 11:2–5 with Deut 17:8–10). Thus the passage gives unique privileges to the royal (later priestly and Levitic) holders of the judicial office in the city: each is not only "judge," but also "one who goes searching for the fitting legal decision but is nevertheless quick in dispensing justice" (16:5).

What gives the law-observant descendants of Jacob, Isaac, Abraham, and even Noah social and religious coherence is a standardized and coherent interpretation of the Law of Moses, which is accepted throughout the diaspora and through successive generations. It is that exposition of the law called *Halakah* which was offered in Jerusalem until the destruction of the city in 70 C.E. and which several generations later was codified in the Mishnah (approx 200 C.E.).

The respect accorded to "strangers," illustrated by 16:1–5, is one of the hallmarks of the Law of Moses (see Exod 20:10; 23:9; Deut 10:17–19). On the other hand, that same law also prohibits the reception of "Ammonite or Moabite" into "the congregation of the Lord" (Deut 23:4–7)! Isaiah 16:1–5 tempers this exclusive attitude, and does so in keeping with the prophet's compassionate spirit and the notion of inclusiveness which, in "A Book of Remembrance" (Genesis–Malachi, as ordered in the Hebrew Bible), balances and counteracts the notion of exclusiveness (see Isa 19:23–25 and 45:20–23).

The Assurance of a Remnant for Moab (16:6–14)

The loss of Moab's prosperous viticulture (6–10) and that people's unanswered appeals to its god Chemosh (12) are prelude to an already looming, more severe fate: the nation's complete ruin "three years" later, leaving only a small and despised remnant (13–14).

The preacher may wish to set the passage into the context of the prophet's concern for the welfare of one's neighbor. The reference to Isaiah's "tears" and "moaning" over Moab's humiliation contrasts with that nation's businesslike dealings with the Israelites on the latter's wilderness journey from Egypt to Canaan. Does not Moses in his farewell speech say that certain Moabites furnished water and food (only) for money (Deut 2:26–29)? By the same token, do not Jewish and Christian ethics stress the mandate of hospitality (58:8; Heb 13:2)?

The Burden of Damascus (17:1–11)

A mere two or three olives visible in the treetop, and four or five left by the pickers in the spreading foliage—this is one of the comparisons of Aram's and Israel's plight after the Assyrian armies have left. In 732 B.C.E. the emperor Tiglathpileser III converted the Kingdom of Syria and the Galilean and Transjordanian parts of the Kingdom of Israel into Assyrian provinces (compare 10:9 and 2 Kings 15:29).

The text relates the near extinction of the monarchy in Samaria to its people's separation from David's house and from the Temple on Zion some two centuries earlier. Did the ten northern tribes, lead by Jeroboam I, at that time not revoke allegiance to the kings of Judah? Did the new king of Israel not make Bethel and Dan—rather than Jerusalem—the sanctuaries of his kingdom? Did the Israelites not build altars throughout their land, appointing non-Levitic priests and instituting a rival celebration of the Feast of Tabernacles (1 Kings 12:1–32)? What is more, did Israel not recently ally itself with the Arameans against their Judaite siblings (2 Kings 16:5), doubling its betrayal? Thus the prophet's "Burden of Damascus" laments not only Syria's fall but also the desertion of "the cities of Aroer," that is, Israel's Transjordanian area. In short, the turmoil of the last decade of the Northern Kingdom (2 Kings 15:8—17:6) provides the backdrop for descriptions of misery and for the announcement of changes to come.

A sermon may deal with other passages in "The Prophets" relating to Damascus, one of the important urban centers of Syria-Palestine throughout the biblical eras (1 Kings 19:15–18; 2 Kings 5:1–27; 8:7–15; Jer 49:23–27; Amos 1:3–5; compare Acts 9:1–22). The preacher notes especially the virtual inclusion of the Arameans, Israel's neighbors and relatives, among those closely related to the Lord (compare Gen 22:21–22 and 25:20). Even Jacob, the father of the twelve tribes of Israel, speaks of himself, at least according to the formulation in Moses' farewell speech (Deut 1—30) as "a wandering Aramean" (Deut 26:5).

Preachers may also explore the lively imagery which describes Israel's and Aram's future. Their condition will be a pitiable one, like that of an emaciated body (4), like a field harvested and then gleaned bare (5), like an olive tree beaten empty by the reapers (6), like a choice garden suddenly wilted (10–11), or like the cities of "Hivites and Amorites" ravaged long ago by the Israelites entering the land (9; compare Num 21:31–35)—the latter nothing less than an inversion of the conquest carried out by the Israelites when they entered the land of promise! But words of hope balance the stern tones: Israel will take its plight to heart, will reject human-made altars, pillars, and idols, will turn to its God and acknowledge the Lord as creator and "the Holy One of Israel" (7–8).

Woes over Assyrians and Cushites (17:12—18:7)

Like wind-driven tumbleweed, the enemies of the Lord's people will quickly disappear from sight while the God of Israel calmly watches their rout. Also in these two "woe!" passages (17:12–14; 18:1–7) vivid comparisons illustrate the certainty of the eventual vindication of Israel and of its divine master.

The first text (17:12–14) does not expressly name the adversaries, but the reference to the roaring multitude of their troops, drawn from many nations, and to their sudden overthrow "from evening to morning" points to the Assyrians. They had overrun Palestine more than once in the last half of the eighth century B.C.E.; their campaign under Sennacherib ended (in 701 B.C.E.) with the loss of many thousands of warriors and the hasty withdrawal of those left alive (17:14; compare 10:28–34; 37:7–8, 36; 14:24–27). The second text (18:1–7) castigates Judah for its mission to Cush, Egypt's southern neighbor, whose land "rivers divide" (evidently the source rivers of the Nile). The Ethiopians are twice described with three unique phrases, one referring to their tall stature and their dark, shiny skin, the second noting their well-known fierceness, and the third pointing to their unswerving pursuit of whatever plans they have made. Yet, though famed and strong, they must not be invited by Judaite envoys into an anti-Assyrian alliance because the God of Israel will overthrow the King of Nineveh without help. By the same token, the rumor of an impending attack of Tirhakah, King of Cush, on the Assyrians (as a result of the Judaite mission?) makes Sennacherib even bolder than his officers in his blasphemy of Israel's God, thus further heightening the greatness of the Lord's anticipated intervention (compare 37:9a with 9b–13 and with 36:4–20).

A sermon may contrast the serenity of Israel's God with the frantic turmoil of surging armies (17:13b/12–13a), or the peaceful arrival of gift-bearing pilgrims from Cush on Mount Zion with the urgent mission of Jerusalem's envoys across the seas in fragile crafts (18:7/2). Moreover, Isaiah envisions elsewhere Egyptians and Cushites coming as bound (?) visitors to Zion, freely acknowledging that the divine presence is found only in its Temple (45:14–17). But also the wide horizons visible to the prophetic eye are manifest: here the powerful king from the upper reaches of the Tigris and there the impressive Africans from the sources of the Nile are both contrasted with the Judaites, a small nation in the hills of Judah. Fittingly, the passage ends with the assurance that those futilely sought as military allies will indeed come, but will do so as pilgrims to "the place of the name of the Lord of Hosts."

The Burden of Egypt (19:1–25)

From the image of the Lord's ride on a swift cloud toward the land of the Nile to the announcement of the divine blessing of Egypt as the Lord's people—an astonishing shift within a mere twenty-five verses! The visionary perspective allows the prophet to move freely through time and space. Thus several political disturbances affecting Egypt in the seventh and sixth centuries B.C.E. are in view, as is the expanse of the ancient Orient: Lower and Upper Egypt, Mesopotamia, as well as Canaan. The text looks forward to five notable changes relating to the Egyptians, specifically the Judaite diaspora in that land at the beginning of the Persian rule. The first part (1b–15) describes the calamities which befall Egypt, while the second (16-25) deals with the new lease on life for the exiled.

The Cloud over Egypt (19:1b-15)

The Lord's arrival in Egypt with a cloud for his chariot (Ps 104:3) strikes both divine and human beings with fear. They hear that it is the Lord's intervention which has brought the disasters of civil war (2), of futile appeal to the gods (3), and of harsh conquerors (4). The failure of the waters of the Nile accompanies the political ruin (5-10)—a rare calamity in a land which is reliably irrigated and sustained by that river. This also reminds the audience of a similar calamity which came over Egypt when another pharaoh refused to let the Lord's people go (compare Exod 6:28—12:36). The counsel of the nation's leaders is of no avail because they fail to recognize that the Lord is at work (11-15; compare 16-22).

A homily may explore the claim that in all events on the world's stage faith can discern the divine hand at work. The heavenly purpose is no respecter of persons and nations. Thus the very words which describe the leaders' loss of control over Egypt are also used to describe the forfeiture of guidance in Israel itself (compare 19:15 with 9:14 and Deut 28:13, 44). The phrase reappears in the castigations of Egypt and Judah because they turn to "soothsayers and diviners" (compare 19:3 with 8:19-20). By the same token, divine acceptance transcends human and national boundaries: the Lord honors Egypt with the title "my people," the very epithet with which Exod 3:7 and 5:1 describe Israel in contrast to its Egyptian oppressors (19:25)!

The Blessing of Egypt (19:16-25)

"On that day. . . . On that day. . . ." No fewer than six times the phrase is used in this text unit—a phrase common in the prophetic writings. What is its import? Does it refer to some day in the future, distant rather than near? Or is its meaning to be derived from its context? The evidence in Isaiah suggests the latter. For instance, the series of four brief "On that day . . ." passages in 7:18-25 refers to the days on which the Assyrian king comes to make war on Israel and Judah (in 722 and 701 B.C.E.). Similarly, the series of the six "On that day ..." texts (19:16–17, 18, 19–20/21–22, 23, 24–25) envisions the days of Egypt's powerlessness in the wake of the Persian conquest and the religious freedom which that rule gives to peoples who had been exiled by Assyrians and Babylonians.

The preacher notes that Isaiah speaks elsewhere of the new opportunities the emperor Cyrus offers to the Judaites and Israelites he found exiled in Mesopotamia (see 44:24—45:8). The text under consideration deals with the displaced Judaites in the lands of the Nile and the new situation which obtains after the Persian king Cambyses, Cyrus' son, has conquered Egypt. In the land of their sojourn they are now at liberty to practice their inherited religion and are even respected by their fellow citizens in their observances (16–17); in fact, five settlements of those loyal to the Lord speak the language of their forebears, "the tongue of Canaan" (18). Moreover, they will erect sanctuaries where sacrifices are offered to Israel's God and where they will find themselves divinely protected (19–22; compare the documents of the Judaite military colony at Elephantine, who in Persian employ guarded the southern border of Upper Egypt; these writings attest the presence of a temple of the Lord in that part of Egypt—in spite of Deuteronomy's insistence that all sacrifices be offered at the one place the Lord chose, presumably Jerusalem). Roads from the Nile and the Euphrates to Mount Zion will be safe for pilgrims; thus worshipers from Egypt will kneel side by side with those from Mesopotamia (23).

The assertion of a divinely blessed harmony that will obtain among the three groups loyal to the Lord concludes the passage: Egypt is honored with the title "people of the Lord"; Assyria, and specifically the Israelites and Judaites domiciled there, is "the work of the Lord's hands"; while "Israel," that is, those who come to the land (of Canaan) as worshipers or settlers, is "the Lord's inheritance" (24–25). The inclusion of the (probably sizable) Egyptian diaspora (compare 30:1–7; 2 Kings 23:34; Jer 41:16—44:30) in the divine ingathering of the servant people Israel (compare 11:11–16; 45:14–17; also Acts 2:5–12) shows that even the threat of a new Egyptian bondage for the disloyal is not (or rather, is no longer?) the last word (contrast Deut 28:64–68).

The Sign for Egypt and Cush (20:1-6)

Isaiah and his disciples are appointed "signs and portents in Israel" (8:11-23a). This passage now proceeds to illustrate how the prophet is ordered to fill that role: for three years before Assyria's defeat of Ashdod (711 B.C.E.) he, on divine order, goes about without cloak and sandals, "naked and barefoot." He relinquishes this mode of dress only when the Assyrian emperor Sargon overthrows the anti-Assyrian alliance of which Ashdod is the head and in which Judah also is participating. At that time he is told to explain his action as harbinger of Egypt's and Cush's future fate: they will go into captivity "naked and barefoot." This indeed happened a generation later when Sennacherib's successor Esarhaddon conquered Egypt (670 B.C.E.), which until that time had been ruled by the Cushite King Tirhakah.

A sermon may explore the prophet's unique role as "sign and portent." The essence of that activity is described in the Exodus stories. There the Lord tells Moses that he will enact many "signs and portents" confounding Pharaoh's hardheartedness (Exod 7:3; compare Deut 4:34). Thus Isaiah, like Moses, carries out the activity appropriate to the message, combining word with gesture so that together they constitute a symbolic action. But while Moses, the archprophet, merely performs signs (Num 12:6-8), Isaiah becomes himself, in his person, "sign and portent." Thus he enacts that prophetic role in a more personal, direct test of the sign: its fulfillment (compare Deut 13:2-6). The narrative of the Egyptian plagues (Exod 6:28—12:36) states and Isa 45:14-17 implies that the signs of both prophets did come true. However, Moses' epitaph in Deut 34:7-12 emphasizes that the signs of Moses shall forever remain unmatched.

The Burden of Sea Wilderness (21:1-10)

The puzzle of the title is solved by the passage: the armies of Elam and Media are called to assail an enemy who plunders and ravages (2), and their attack leads to the fall of Babylon (9). Thus it is Nebuchadnezzar's mighty empire whose ruin the prophet envisions. This is a second "burden" which relates to Babylon—evidence of that nation's importance in

Isaiah's view (compare the first "burden" in 13:1—14:23). Only one other nation receives double treatment: Assyria (14:24-27; 17:12—18:7). These two superpowers successively "made world politics" in the two centuries which the prophet's horizon spans (approx. 750–540 B.C.E.).

The preacher notes the stylistic complexity of the passage but also the urgency of "the harsh vision" given to the prophet. Thus the text weaves together Isaiah's words of description (1b–2a), four kinds of quotation, and finally his own reaction. The quotations are composed of the Lord's own words (2b, 6–8a, 10) and even of a quotation by the Lord of a watchman's future statement (7–8a), of the orders given by the Babylonian commanders (5), and finally of the messengers' calls announcing (to Zion) Babylon's fall (9b; compare 52:7–10). The prophet's reactions are expressed in cries of pain over the great city's misery (3–4) and finally in the assurance of his own constant watchfulness in his prophetic role (8b–9a).

The text's weighty theme corresponds to its artful shaping. It describes the coming overthrow of the powerful metropolis, brought about by its eastern neighbors under the leadership of the Persian king, Cyrus, whom 45:1–8 will introduce by name and honor with the title "the Lord's anointed one." Already "the Burden of Babylon" (13:1—14:23) had made that very announcement; its repetition in 21:1–10 demonstrates that it is indeed wrought by the Lord (compare Gen 41:[1–]32). In the third part of Isaiah (38—55) that prediction made by the God of Israel is many times presented as the ultimate proof of the Lord's supremacy: was it not the Lord—and no other god—who "declared from the beginning" the coming of "a victorious one from the East" (41:25–29; compare 41:21–24; 45:1–8, 8–13; 46:8–13)? But 21:1–10 also stresses the prophet's constant alertness to the divine presence as a condition for receiving visionary insight (8b).

The Burden of Dumah (21:11–12)

During the daytime the watchmen of camps and cities are on the lookout for attackers (compare 2 Kings 9:17). At night they are the ones who are able to tell "how much is left of the night" (11b), presumably by their observation of the stars.

This text casts the prophet into the role of such a watchman. He is asked by a voice coming from (the Mount of) Seir, where the Edomites live (Gen 36:20), how far the night has advanced. He responds that daylight has already appeared on the eastern horizon, but that it is nevertheless still night. He concludes that a second, later enquiry is in order.

Discussions of the prophet's role as watchman over nations are found elsewhere in "The Prophets" (see Ezek 33:1–20 and Jer 1:4–10). However, these texts do not seem to illuminate our text, which remains obscure on other counts. Possibly it anticipates the future rout of Edom as described in 34:(1)5–17 (compare 11:14 and 63:1–6).

The Burden of Arabia (21:13–17)

Sprung from Abraham and Hagar, the Arab tribes of Nebaioth, Kedar, and Tema are close relatives of Isaac's and Jacob's descendants (see Gen 25:12–16). As caravaneers and animal breeders they frequent the oases of the desert to the south and the east of Canaan; then, as now, they are famous for their hospitality.

The text "the Burden of Arabia" laments their inability to be faithful to that tradition: they are no more able to meet wayfarers with food and drink. It is the ruin which the armies of the Mesopotamian superpowers brought over their region which has made them refugee wayfarers themselves. Thus Kedar will share the fate of Moab, Judah, Israel, and Tyre: only a small remnant will be left (see 16:13–14; 6:12–13; 14:1–2; 23:15–18). However, the survivors of Kedar will also participate in the celebration of the Lord's restoration of Zion: with shouts of joy and choice animals they will arrive at the Temple in Jerusalem (42:10–12; 60:4–7). Do they not also claim Abraham as their ancestor and are they not therefore invited into the covenant of the Lord's peace (compare 51:2 and 55:1–13; also Gen 16:9–10 and 2:12–13)?

The Burden of Vision Valley (22:1–25)

"What is the matter with you?" Twice (1b, 15) this provocative question begins a sharp reprimand. The first condemns the complacency of "Vision Valley" in the face of siege and threatening defeat (1b–14); the second chastises the arrogant behavior of one of the high royal officials (15–25). The reproaches, stylistically aligned through their identical opening lines, are addressed to inhabitants of "Vision Valley," the first to all its citizenry, the second only to an individual.

The identity of the addressee is clarified by two features of the text: the four measures taken to strengthen its defenses (8b–11a), and the mention of the officer's name (15). They both indicate that Hezekiah's Jerusalem is intended. The metaphoric name probably alludes to the city's location, largely in the Kidron Valley between Mount Zion to the west and the Mount of Olives to the east. It is there that the prophet receives the visions which are brought together into "the vision to Isaiah," that is, Isa 1—66 (compare 6:1–13 and 29:11). A similar figurative designation appears in 21:1–10, where Babylon is introduced as "Sea Wilderness."

Jerusalem's Pride (22:1b–14)

The intensity of the prophetic thought shapes the passage. The threat to the city of Jerusalem posed by Sennacherib's army in 701 B.C.E. (5:26–29; 10:28–29, 30–32; and 36:1–3) is perceived through the visionary medium as merely the beginning of the city's troubles. While the Assyrian menace was removed by divine intervention, leaving it intact (37:8, 22b–35, 36–38), several generations later the Babylonian attackers actually succeeded in conquering and destroying the city with its temple and palace (compare 39:6–9; 2 Kings 24:10–16; 25:1–21). The descriptions of Jerusalem's ruin in 2b–3 and 5–8a seem to relate to that second, more dire fate come over Jerusalem at the hands of Nebuchadnezzar. On the other hand, the four measures undertaken to strengthen the city's defenses, especially the repair of the wall and the installation of a conduit safeguarding the water supply are King Hezekiah's achievements (compare 2 Kings 20:20 and 2 Chron 32:1–5, 30).

The preacher notes the seemingly thoughtless indulgence of the city dwellers, expressed in the memorable phrase, "Let us eat and drink, for tomorrow we die!" (13). Reprehensible though the words are, they are not different in outlook from Hezekiah's reaction to Isaiah's words: when the prophet announces the future exile of the monarch's descendants to Babylonian court service, the king shrugs the prediction off with the thought that there will at least be peace during his lifetime (39:1–8). Does not the longer view of prophets (and apostles, compare 1 Cor 15:32) offer a deeper, more penetrating understanding of the events which occupy both history and human minds? The parable in 28:23–29 compares the goal orientation and labor differentiation of the farmer with the manner of the Lord's action, and the prophetic perspective, encompassing many generations and places, perceives "a vision of the whole" (29:11).

Shebna's Boast (22:15–25)

Rolled up turban and pulled out wall peg—the passage is full of action and suspense. King Hezekiah's vizier Shebna had a pretentious rock tomb cut for himself and his family in the Kidron Valley, readily visible from the city (an imposing tomb structure, erected in a later period, may still be seen there today). Contrary to Shebna's assumption that his exalted position at court is secure, the prophet addresses him with the announcement, not only of his removal from office and banishment to another place, but also of the appointment of Eliakim, son of Hilkiah, in his place. Shebna and his large family will be left broken and in disarray, like an assortment of pots and pans whose weight has pulled from the wall the peg on which they had been hanging.

The preacher notes that a certain Shebna is mentioned again in 36:3. There he is the second of three cabinet members whom Hezekiah sends to meet the Assyrian commander who has been dispatched to the city by Sennacherib from Lachish (compare 2 Kings 18:13–18). In this text Eliakim is mentioned before Shebna and identified as vizier, the position from which Shebna has been demoted. Thus the prophetic predictions of 22:17–19 and 24–25 have not been fulfilled, at least by this time, in their severity. A similar less stringent realization of a divine prediction is found already at the beginning of the Bible: was not disobedient Adam merely banned from the divine presence, contrary to the prediction that "on that day" on which he transgresses "he will die" (compare Gen 2:17 with 3:17–19)?

On the other hand, a sermon may explore the theme of the

downfall of arrogance, and do so with reference to comparable texts in "The Prophets." There the replacement of an officeholder found to be lacking in faith in the God of Israel is told several times. Thus the last Omride king, Joram, is removed from kingship, primarily because of his father Ahab's arrogance, and Jehu, son of Nimshi, takes his place at the Lord's bidding (2 Kings 9:6–10). Similarly, the position of Eli, the priest in Shiloh's sanctuary during the time of King Saul, is taken from his house and given to Zadok, a priest loyal to the Lord (1 Sam 2:27–36; compare 1 Kings 2:26–27). So also David, son of Jesse, replaces Saul, son of Kish (1 Sam 15:10–28). The proverb puts it succinctly: "Comes pride, comes disgrace" (Prov 11:2).

The Burden of Tyre (23:1–18)

Oceangoing vessels that wail, refugees who wander without finding a place to rest, a harlot who must endure ridicule because her graces have wilted and she has fallen from favor—the imagery reflects the cosmopolitan air of the renowned city of the Phoenicians. As seafearers and traders of the Mediterranean during the two and a half centuries dealt with by Isaiah (approximately 750–500 B.C.E.), they were well known in the ancient world and thus also to the Israelites and Judaites. Generations ago King Hiram of Tyre had been allied with King Solomon, supplying timber and craftsmen for the erection of temple and palace in Jerusalem (1 Kings 5:15–25 [RSV: 5:1–11]; 7:13; and 40). Then, in the ninth century B.C.E. the Sidonian Princess Jezebel became Israel's King Ahab's queen, and a generation later their daughter Athaliah was queen and despot of Jerusalem (1 Kings 16:31; 2 Kings 8:18; 11:1–20). The prophetic writings are well informed about Tyre's international citizenry and its impressive variety of merchandise (compare Ezek 26:1—28:19; Amos 1:9–10; and Zech 9:3–4).

The preacher notes the breadth of the prophet's perspective, excelled only by Ezekiel's full-blown descriptions. "Tarshish-Ships" are symbols of Phoenician mercantile success. It seems that they were so named because they were able to make the long journey to "Tarshish," the places in Sardinia and/or Spain where copper and tin were mined, refined, and sold. These vessels were used to import grain from Egypt (3); their failure to carry on such enterprise harms the economy of that country (5). The news of the straits in which Tyre finds itself has reached other ports, unnerving the Phoenician crews and keeping them from setting sail for home (1, 14).

Isaiah's word presents Babylonia's defeat of Assyria—Nineveh fell in 612 B.C.E.—as example to Tyre, illustrating the manner in which the self-confident will fall (13; compare 4). However, there is no ancient evidence, except for the prophet's words, that ancient Tyre was conquered before Alexander's campaigns. On the other hand, Nebuchadnezzar did lay siege to the city for some thirteen years; 23:1–14 probably refers to this threat as "devastation." The announcement of the city's restoration after "seventy years" (17) is not attested elsewhere in Scripture or ancient Oriental literature and is in this respect comparable to the similarly unattested "seventy years' " desertion of Jerusalem (see Jer 25:11–12).

A sermon may deal with the prophetic insistence that Tyre's fate must be understood as the work of the God of Israel (8–9, 18). In words reminiscent of Moses' "stretching his hand over the sea," of the Lord's subsequent "shaking" of kingdoms and nations, and of Israel's eventual conquest of Canaan, events of Isaiah's time are conceived as repetition or continuation of what began long ago (compare 11 with Exod 14:15–31 and 15:14–15). By the same token, the dedication of gifts brought from far and near for the Lord's service is the climax of the divine ingathering not only, as of old, from the land of the Nile, but now also from the four corners of the earth, even from as far away as Tarshish (compare 18 with 11:11–16; 18:7; 60:4–9; and 66:18–20).

The Banquet for All the Nations (24:1—27:13)

The rout of Babylonia and Assyria, Moab and Syria, Israel and Judah, Egypt and Cush, Arabia and Tyre (13:1—23:18) is perceived as the work of no other than the God of Israel (compare 14:26–27). But this is not Isaiah's last word concerning the nations; the following texts bring words of hope and blessing.

The segment 24:1—27:13 attests the prophetic persuasion that a radical transformation of the world is the setting not only of the Lord's royal rule on Mount Zion (24:1–23), but also of the invitation extended to all nations to come and feast on the holy mountain (25:1—26:6). More, the prophet proceeds to speak of the planting and rooting of the Lord's "vineyard of delight," which reaches out into the world yet remains centered in the Lord's worship in Jerusalem (26.7—27:13).

In short, in Isa 24—27 the overall thematic composition of Isaiah appears: the move from chastisement to consolation, from reproach to promise. Thus Isa 24—27 fits into the thematic master structure of the book and is interpreted here in light of this conceptual coherence. The following interpretation does not isolate 24—27 from the rest of the book nor employ the title "Isaiah Apocalypse"; on the other hand, the "apocalyptic" flavor of the passage will call for comment.

The Transformation of Heaven and Earth (24:1–23)

A bewildering array of pictures meets the eye: the earth laid bare and twisted, mistress and slave girl become equals, timbrels and lyres silenced, heavenly windows opened, foundations of the world shaken, even moon and sun eclipsed. Moreover, jarring word repetitions (3, 8, 16, 19) create a staccato rhythm and suggest great urgency, driving to the poem's climax: the celebration of Israel's God as king in Zion, surrounded by a world overturned. Small wonder that the text's heaven- and earth-embracing perspective and its memorable imagery continue to impress themselves on readers as examples of what has come to be known as "apocalyptic writing."

What uniquely characterizes this and similar compositions is their relation to the opening chapters of the Bible: the stories and motifs of cosmic origins and cataclysms (Gen 1—11) reappear but in muted, veiled, or heightened fashion, their scriptural order replicated or inverted. By the same token, sustained "apocalyptic" passages may conclude biblical books or sections of books. Thus 24—27 concludes the book's first part; similarly, the vision of "a new heaven and a new earth" is the climax of the epilogue of the book (see 65:15–25 and 66:1–24). Other examples are Ezek 40:1—48:35 (esp. 47:1–12), Zech 12:1—14:21 (esp. 14:6–9), Mark 13:1–37, and Rev 19:11—22:5). What characterizes many such "closure"

Isaiah 5:1—27:13   81

texts is their sometimes mirrorlike correspondence to the
"opener" texts of the larger literary context to which they belong. They seek to "redo" what has been "undone" before. In
this fashion they create through counterimaging a sense of
both dialectical tension and balancing harmony.

The preacher notes the universal dimensions of the earth's
upset. It is first described broadly (1–3), then spelled out in
some detail (4–13). The kings from Nineveh and Babylon conquered, or at least threatened, all regions of the eastern Mediterranean world for some two centuries (approximately 745–
538 B.C.E.). Indeed, they did change the face of that world rad-
ically. Not only did their system of provinces supplant the
small kingdoms of Syria-Palestine (1), but also their repeated
deportations of parts of the populace leveled in status "priest
and layperson," commoner and aristocrat (2). Furthermore,
the tributes they exacted from vassals, not to mention the
treasures they took from the vanquished, left the lands deso-
late (3, 4–13).

However, the respect and tolerance of the Persian rulers for
the religious traditions of the peoples whom they had subdued allowed displaced worshipers of the Lord (as of other
deities) to raise their heads and to let their voices of praise
once again be heard. Now the exiles can call to Jerusalem
from the East and the West with words of encouragement for
the loyal (14–16a). Just the same, the prophet must lament
bitterly the devastation of the lands at home and abroad
(16b–20) and also assert that the fall of the powerful and their
consignment to the underworld (22; compare 14:3–21) will
"on that day" manifest the royal rule of the Lord on Mount
Zion (21–23).

A sermon may explore the correspondence between the
text's universal ("apocalyptic") motifs and their counterparts
in "A Book of Remembrance" (Genesis–Malachi, as ordered
in the Hebrew Bible). The allusions to the deluge story (Gen
5:5—9:17) and to the two stories of creation (Gen 1:2—2:4a;
2:4b–25) are especially noteworthy. Thus "the opening of the
(celestial) windows" (18) corresponds to the other use of that
phrase in Gen 7:11 and 8:2, where it refers to the Lord's un-
locking of the apertures of the firmament, letting the heavenly waters inundate the terrestrial sphere to the point where

chaos threatens to return. But while Gen 7:11 and 8:2 pair the phrase with "the welling of the springs of the deep," Isa 24:18 juxtaposes it to "the shaking of the earth's foundations." These two phrases suggest that the overthrow of the ancient Orient by Assyrians and Babylonians is "deluge-like," that is, not only far-reaching as Noah's Flood, but also anticipating a new and different terrestrial age in the same manner as did that deluge of old (compare also 54:4–10).

The darkening of moon and sun in the Lord's presence (23), on the other hand, is another "closure" theme. It points to the primacy of the divine radiance outshining the luminaries of the firmament which run their fixed courses and were called into being only on the fourth day of the creation (Gen 1:2—2:4a; especially 14–18; 2:1). Hence sun and moon are unrelated to the primal radiance; they are secondary and temporary (compare 60:19–20; Zech 14:6–7; Mark 13:24–25 [which quote Isa 13:10 and 34:4] and Rev 22:5). The God of Israel, whom Isaiah's disciples worship, is thus in sovereign command of sun and moon; they are subdued and in due time remembered in accord with the divine will (22).

The Transformation of Mount Zion (25:1—26:6)

A bountiful banquet on Mount Zion where a veil covering the nations is removed, tears wiped away, and even death swallowed up—the words soar to heights almost without parallel in Isa 1—66. A prayer by the prophet begins the text (25:1–5). It is followed by three announcements of what the seer envisions "on that day": a feast on the holy hill celebrated by all the nations (25:6–8), their solemn affirmation of the Lord as "our God" (25:9–12), and the recitation of the song of the land of Judah, inviting the pilgrims to enter Jerusalem's gates (26:1–6). The notion of Zion as the center of the terrestrial sphere has already been introduced in the preceding passage (24:23). This image will also form the conclusion of the following text (27:12–13).

The preacher notes that the prophet's prayer (25:1–5) recognizes the Lord as Isaiah's personal God, thus highlighting the direct relationship initiated by the prophet's vision in the Temple (6:1–13) and affirmed by the call to Isaiah's disciples to separate themselves from their contemporaries for exclusive devotion to their divine Lord (8:11–23a). The words of the prayer proceed to contrast the fall of Babylon, never to be rebuilt (compare 25:2 with 14:22–23; 21:9), with the exaltation of Zion as "shelter from the torrent, shade from the heat" (compare 25:4b with 4:6).

The intriguing announcement of "The Great Banquet on Mount Zion" (25:6–8) discloses what all the nations coming to Jerusalem as pilgrims or settlers will find there: not only the choicest of food and drink, but also full access to the divine presence (see also Matt 8:5–13). Fittingly, the remainder of the passage consists of quotations of what will be said by various persons "on that day." One is a prayer spoken in celebration of the Lord as "our God," who is present on this mountain, but who also lays low neighboring Moab (25:9–12). The other is the invitation extended to those loyal to the God of Israel to enter confidently Jerusalem's gates for worship and feasting (26:1–6).

Finally, a sermon may explore the relation of the Great Feast on Zion's hill to the primal, universal story of the Garden of Eden (Gen 2:4b—3:24) and the manner in which Isa 25:6–8 inverts it. The verbal imagery is similar enough to establish a connection but also sufficiently different to suggest the rite of pilgrimage. The inversion is evident in the contrast between "expulsion" here and "invitation" there: the call to "all" nations overcomes the exile of Adam and Eve, the primal parents of humankind. The offer of fine food, even of wine, recalls the similar though restricted supply of sustenance in the Garden of Eden. The promise of the removal of mortality recalls the divine threat of death as the result of human disobedience, then as "on that day" related to the consumption of the divinely proffered food. However, not the infliction of death but the eviction of the first parents was in fact the divine action prompted by Eve's and Adam's failure to observe the prohibition. It was that act of disloyalty which placed them outside Paradise and deprived them of that fullness of life which had been their birthright. The grief and the dishonor which their action brought them correspond to the removal of tears and shame announced in 25:8 (compare Gen 3:23–24).

Other passages in Isaiah speak of the prosperity, blessing,

and joy which are the marks of "Zion Restored" (compare 11:1–16; 35:8–10; 54:1–3; 60:1–22; and 65:15–25). In fact, the Lord's compassion for Zion is such that "he made its (once) waste (places) like Eden, its ruin like the Garden of the Lord" (51:3). In keeping with this affirmation another prophet envisions a river of life-giving water issuing from underneath the altar near the Temple, turning sterile stretches of land into fertile regions (Ezek 47:1–12). By the same token, the Law of Moses describes the most holy place of the divine presence as shielded by a cherubim-patterned veil and guarded by the continual altar fire (compare Exod 26:31–33 and Lev 6:2 with Gen 3:24).

The Transformation of Israel (26:7—27:13)

Not only Mount Zion, not only heaven and earth will be made new (24:1–23; 25:1—26:6), but also Israel, the Lord's vineyard. The prophetic words move from reflection to prayer and from exhortation to visionary anticipation, transposing the audience into its meditative state of mind. (By the way, that mode of speaking makes for phrases and whole lines which are difficult to understand—one modern version [NJV] identifies no fewer than eight "uncertain" lines!). Broadly speaking, the text advances, like other Isaianic passages, from words of chastisement (26:10–11, 13, 17–18, 20–21) to assurances of hope (26:15, 19; 27:2–6, 12–13). Its first unit is based on the prophet's meditation on Israel's apostasy and the Lord's loyalty (26:7–19); the second one (26:20–27:13), after an introduction, lays out the nature of the divine intervention "on that day."

Prophetic Meditation (26:7–19)

The reflective mood allows the prophetic voice not only stylistic freedom but also the exploration of intimate thoughts: members of the Isaianic circle "yearn during the night and into the morning" for the manifestation of their divine Lord's greatness (compare 9 with Ps 1:2). They ask themselves: Does the Lord's magnanimity toward the disobedient not confirm these people in their apostasy (10; compare Mal 3:13–21)? But the disciples must also observe that divine forbearance of idolaters, for instance, as portrayed in Exodus–Numbers or Judges, illustrates the dilemma: the Lord's chastisement may bring Israel back to its divine master but does so for the length of a generation at best (compare 15–18 with Judg 2:6–19). On the other hand, the expectation of the Lord's eventual gift of new life, even to those already deceased, is the climax of the prophetic meditation (19; compare 25:8).

A sermon may explore this example of religious reflection, its mode, its theme, its manifestation, and its life-affirming result. The "soul" of prophetic followers, like that of their master, "longs" for the Lord's "name and remembrance." That pining fills them continuously, even during their hours of sleep. The object of meditation is the Lord's "judgments"—divine intervention on Israel's behalf, whether castigation or deliverance (8–9). Their thoughts fasten on those who persist in apostasy, in contrast with others who remain loyal. Offering "cheap grace" to the former is of little avail (10–11, compare 7). Nevertheless, even though "foreign masters ruled" over Israel, the Lord's presence is certainly with the faithful (12–15). To be sure, prophets are not able to do what only Israel's God can do; they are and will remain merely "signs and portents" in the land (16–18; compare 8:18).

The meditation concludes with the assurance that renewed life, a veritable resurrection, is the portion of "the Lord's dead," as it is of the prophet's own corpse. In exuberance "the dwellers of the dust" can now be commanded to rise and to rejoice (19). Here the interpreter is reminded of another prophet's vision of new life given to dry bones (Ezek 37:1–14), not to mention the assurance living within many Jews and Christians ever since that the resurrection and the judgment of the dead is prelude to the divine restoration of all creation to its primal glory (compare Dan 12:2–3 [OT]; 2 Macc 6:10–11 [Septuagint/Apocrypha]; John 5:24–29; 1 Cor 15:50–57 [NT]; Sot 9:15 and Sanh 10:1 [Mishnah]).

Prophetic Anticipation (26:20—27:13)

Leviathan vanquished, Israel spreading throughout the inhabited world, a great trumpet sounding—the images are memorable! The prophet's vision of the Lord's transformation transcends space and time: Mesopotamia and Egypt are in view, as is the plight of Israel's scattered remnants. The latter are counseled (26:20–21) to withdraw into the safety of their small settlements, there to wait out the deluge-like storm unleashed in the world through the defeats of two superpowers by their successors: Babylonia overpowered Assyria (Nineveh fell in 612 B.C.E.), only to be struck down itself by the Persians (Babylon fell in 539 B.C.E.). Now the seclusion of what later became "ghettos" must provide cover and ensure survival.

The four following paragraphs describe in detail the world's transformation "on that day," that is, after the victory of King Cyrus. First, the Lord's all-powerful sword visits "Leviathan, the elusive serpent" (Assyria?), "Leviathan, the twisting serpent" (Babylonia?), as well as "the Dragon of the sea" (Egypt?) (see 27:1; compare 7–11). These unique names of monsters may be those of mythic sea creatures of which pre-biblical, ancient Canaanite texts from the Phoenician port city of Ugarit (northern Syria) speak. Second, Israel as the Lord's restored vineyard not only brings forth the fruit expected of its first planting (compare 5:1–7), but sends its tendrils and branches as far as its dispersed members are scattered throughout the inhabited world (27:2–6). Third, loyal Israelites who long to return to the land of their ancestors and to settle there are individually called back from the valleys of the Nile, the Tigris, and the Euphrates (27:12). Finally, observant descendants of Jacob-Israel are summoned by the assembly call of "a great trumpet" to make the pilgrimage to Jerusalem, the Lord's holy mountain (27:13).

The preacher may base a homily on the inclusiveness which informs the text. The conclusion of the first part of Isaiah (5:1–27:13) returns to the comprehensive perspective with which the book itself and the Hebrew Bible both begin and end. The correspondence between "opener" and "closure" texts may be seen in the references to "heaven and earth," 1:2 and Gen 1:3–2:4a, as well as 65:17–20/66:22–23 and Rev 21:1 (compare also the discussion of frameworks in the Introduction). By the same token, Israel as the Lord's vineyard is not only made new but also transformed into a worldwide community. It is present wherever descendants of Jacob, of Isaac, of Abraham, even of Noah choose to observe the Law of Moses as the divine order of life and turn to Jerusalem in prayer and in pilgrimage (27:2-6, 12-13; compare Deut 30:15-20 and Dan 6:11).

Moreover, the appearance of the guideword "vineyard" in 5:1-7 and 27:2-6, framing the book's first part and suggesting its lead theme, invites comparison of the two texts. Of old, Israel failed to bring forth good fruit, but the new Israel produces choice wine. The first vineyard lost the good will of its lord, but the new planting is well watered and continuously guarded. Thorns and thistles overgrew the old garden, but the divine master will remove the plants of curse and sterility from the new, should they threaten to take over the beloved plantation. Israel of old was full of iniquity and cries of the oppressed, but the new Israel is doubly secured by the Lord's gift of peace. Finally, the planting of yore was confined by hedge and wall, but the Israel of the prophet's vision covers the face of the earth with its yield. Small wonder that the vineyard theme, central in Isa 1—66, appears elsewhere in the Bible as well (see Jer 12:10-17; 1 Kings 21:1-24; Mark 12:1-12; and John 15:1-8).

PART 2
The Vision of Assyria's Withdrawal and Jerusalem's Rescue
(Isaiah 28:1—37:38)

In this part of Isa 1—66 the prophet's vision fastens on Jerusalem's escape from a threatened Assyrian conquest. In 701 B.C.E. Sennacherib attacked the city but later withdrew without taking it. While the first section (28:1—35:10) anticipates that assault, the second (36:1—37:38) describes it in detail. On the other hand, the second part of Isa 1—66 parallels that rescue of the city to the one described in its first part (5:1–27:13). That earlier aggression had occurred when the Ephraimite-Syrian alliance failed to capture Jerusalem and to force King Ahaz to make common cause with Aram and Israel against Assyria. By the same token, the book's second part also sets the stage for its third (38:1—55:13); there the prophetic vision focuses on Babylon's fall and the new lease on life granted to Zion when it was rebuilt by those who had been allowed to return from exile.

The Lord's Call to Feasting in Zion (28:1—35:10)

From chastisement to encouragement—this section also is structured in accord with the compositional pattern found throughout Isa 1—66 (see the discussion in the Introduction). Six reproaches (28:1—33:9) are followed by the vision of "Zion, the city of our festivals" (33:20) and of "the holy road" (35:8) on which the pilgrims stream to the city (33:10—35:10). Has not the divine rescue of Jerusalem from the Assyrian threat in 701 B.C.E. (30:29–31; 31:8–9; compare 36:1—37:38 / 2 Kings 18:13—19:37) demonstrated that the Lord does indeed protect Zion, his holy mountain (31:4–5)?

The Woes over the Lord's Adversaries (28:1—33:9)

Six times the lament cry "woe!" introduces a castigation of those who ignore or oppose the Lord's claims. The units address different groups: the first (28:1-29) reproaches the elite of Samaria and Jerusalem, while the second (29:1-14) deals with the people and the prophets of "Ariel" (Zion). The third (29:15-24) castigates those who belittle the Lord's word. The fourth and the fifth (30:1-33; 31:1—32:20) counter persons who turn to Egypt for refuge or help, while the last (33:1-9) begins by addressing "a plunderer not (yet) plundered," presumably Assyria. The passages are directed to different though overlapping groups and vary in both length and argumentation. All are conceived as aspects of the prophet's far-ranging "vision of the whole" (29:11). Interpreters note that the first part of Isa 1—66 also contains a series of six "woes!" (5:8-24). That sequence of texts reproaches, like its counterpart in 28:1—33:9, those who reject the Lord's instruction. Both series are polemics against those who "err in spirit" (29:24b), that is, persons who in either attitude or behavior reject the prophet's standards. In short, the two "woe!" series may be read as examples of biblical heresiologies.

The "Woe!" over Ephraim and Judah (28:1-29)

The passage presents intriguing images. It moves from "the proud crown of the drunkards of Ephraim" and the puzzling repetition of short syllables to the notion of the Lord's "strange work" and "astonishing manner of action." Moreover, the text contains varied comparisons drawn from agriculture (4, 24-28), and a graphic description of the results of drunkenness (8), but also cryptic references to monosyllables said over and over again (19, 13), and an emphatic description of a stone deposited in a special location and readied for a crucial function (16). The prophet's vision moves freely from one group to another, from quotation to proverb—evidence of the wide horizons of the passage. The first paragraph (1-6) chastises Ephraim's elite, the second (7-22) subjects Judah's ruling class to even more searing reproach, while the third (23-

29) discourses in parable fashion on the goal orientation and labor differentiation of the Lord's counsel and action.

The Future of Ephraim's Remnant (28:1–6)

The prophetic eye turns to the ruling class of the Northern Kingdom, whose capital Samaria is located "at the head of a fat valley," that is, overlooking the fertile basin from within which it rises to commanding height (1, 4; compare 1 Kings 16:24). A people's elite easily falls prey to arrogance, especially when the luxuries of the privileged are readily available. 28:1–22 shows that the upper classes of neither Israel nor Judah escaped that fate. Of the two, the Northern Kingdom (Israel) was brought low first. In 733 B.C.E. its northern areas (Golan Heights and Galilee) were incorporated into the Assyrian provincial system (compare 7:1–6; 9:1–4; 2 Kings 15:29), and some ten years later what had remained as a rump kingdom around its capital Samaria suffered the same fate (compare 9:7—10:4 and 2 Kings 15:8—17:6).

The preacher notes that the Assyrian defeat of Israel is compared to what happens to an early ripening fig when a passerby spots and in an instant plucks and devours it (4). However, this is not the last word. A word of hope for Ephraim is also sounded. The Lord will eventually become Israel's glory; that is, Israel's remnant will turn to Jerusalem, where the divine presence may be celebrated, the Law of Moses heard, and fellow pilgrims met (compare 14:1–2 and Jer 41:4–5).

The Reproach of Jerusalem's Arrogance (28:7–22)

Vomit on tables, tedious repetition of short syllables, a covenant made with death, and the deposit of a testing stone in Jerusalem—here also intriguing images, here also the move from condemnation to promise. The passage, born of the prophet's reflection, makes manifest the tension which the withdrawal of the prophetic circle from their contemporaries (8:11–23a) creates.

Priest as well as prophet are found to be unfit because their ill-disciplined indulgence in fermented drink makes them fail in their appointed tasks. Does not traditional law expressly prohibit priests on duty from consuming intoxicants (compare 7 and 12 with Lev 10:8–11)? But those reprimanded reject condescendingly the prophet's reproach. As far as they are concerned, what the prophet says is at best comparable to the instruction which little children receive when they learn the alphabet, "a little here, a little there." The repeated syllables (10:13) are reminiscent of the words for "precept" and "standard" or "rule"; also, they begin with the consonants ṣ and q which occur in this order and follow each other in the Hebrew alphabet. The prophet counters that the priests shirk their duty and so fail to offer "respite to the weary," that is, the rendering of legal and cultic decision when called upon to do so. Contrary to the priestly claims of having secured for themselves and their contemporaries escape from death, the prophet speaks of the Lord's unexpected and "strange" intervention which will bring a new standard of justice as well as complete ruin to those who persist in opposition.

The preacher may wish to explore the notion of the Lord's "strange deed" of setting up in Jerusalem a "testing stone." Even though 7–22 is cryptic in some of its allusions, it looks toward a divine intervention introducing a "touchstone," that is, a semiprecious stone such as black jasper, used in antiquity to determine the degree of purity of silver or gold by examining the coloring of scratch marks made with the metal on the stone's surface. The new standard also supersedes the addressees' "covenants with death and the underworld" (18; compare 15); in other words, it offers life rather than death. Alerted by similar passages in Isaiah such as 2:2–5 and 11:1–9, the interpreter is led to think of King Josiah's introduction (in 622 B.C.E.) of "the book of the law (of Moses)" (Deut 30:10; compare Josh 23:6). That sustained, highly focused work is (essentially) Deuteronomy, which presents itself as the parting Moses' final and comprehensive summary of laws already given to Israel (collected in Exodus–Numbers). It is Moses' testament to Israel. Kept by the Levites near the ark of the covenant and copied for royal study (Deut 31:9–13; 17:14–20), Deuteronomy seeks to insure uniformity in the administration of justice; it attempts to cover all legal cases which may arise in the worldwide community of Judaism and be brought to Jerusalem for arbitration (17, 20; compare Deut

16:18–20 and 17:8–13). Moreover, does not Moses' final word emphasize the offer of blessing and life as climax and goal (compare 15 and 18 with Deut 28:1–14; 30:15–20; and 32:46–47)? In other words, the "touchstone" refers to the standard which Deuteronomy claims to be.

The touchstone motif of Isa 28:16 is important in several early Christian writings. In some Jesus is seen, in keeping with the testing stone motif, as a new standard; thus those who take offense at him test themselves, as it were, out of the community of the faithful (see Rom 9:33 and 10:11). On the other hand, the combination of the stone motif of Isa 28 with that of another noteworthy stone, the cornerstone of Ps 118:22, leads to the presentation of Jesus as the foundation stone of a new, spiritual temple, into which the faithful are fitted as "living stones" (1 Peter 2:6; compare Eph 2:20).

The Parable of the Farmer (28:23–29)

Like a wandering philosopher the prophet appeals to the audience. The hearers' interest is aroused with rhetorical questions; the answers persuade them to affirm what the farmer's work demonstrates: in both seedtime and harvest the work must be carefully planned, properly timed, and conscientiously executed, marked by goal orientation, labor differentiation, and appropriate tool selection. No step is left out, nothing done in excess, and everything in due time.

The description not only is interesting in its own right as a glimpse into ancient horticulture, it also points to a divine order as the source of such measured and targeted action (26,29). But does the text teach only that? What is its purpose in the context of the prophet's six "woe!" passages (28:1—33:16)? Expressly formulated as the prophet's own composition, it explains in parabolic form his theological argument. It is this: the many and varied vicissitudes to which the Lord's people find themselves subjected, especially by the repeated threats to palace, temple, city, and nation, are in fact aspects of the Lord's wisdom and counsel in dealing with Israel, the Lord's people. "The vision of the whole" (29:11; compare 6:1–13 and 22:11b; also Introduction) enables Isaiah to perceive what others do not: the Lord's long-range plan of repeated chastisement of Israel, leading them through suffering and testing to eventual restoration and blessing (compare Deut 8:1–5 for a similar argument).

The "Woe!" over Ariel (29:1–14)

The second "woe!" passage in the series of some six (28:1—33:16) is addressed to "Ariel, the city where David camped," in other words, to Jerusalem (see 2 Sam 23:20). While the first "woe!" text (28:1–29) castigates Zion's priests and prophets for their abuse of "fermented drink and wine," the second again deals with their intoxication but "not through wine and fermented drink" (compare 28:7–8 with 29:9)! Now Isaiah speaks of their spiritual blindness, evident in their mechanical observation of festal calendar and cultic rite (1, 13–14)—a theme already introduced in the prologue (1:2—4:6). There the passage dealing with "the peril of selective obedience" (1:10–20) rejects conformance with cultic obligations which is not accompanied by the fulfillment of equally demanded social duties, notably, equitable treatment of orphan and widow. By the same token, in the book's epilogue (56:1—66:24) one text unit castigates those who meticulously observe fasts but neither let the oppressed go free nor share their food with the hungry (58:1–7).

The preacher notes that the first paragraph (1–8) describes both a future siege of the city (1–4) and its sudden termination (5–6), so that the beleaguered may ignore the attacking army as one puts aside an unwelcome dream (7–8). This refers to the unexpected end of the Assyrian siege in 701 B.C.E., announced, to be sure, by the prophet beforehand and greeted by the city with surprise and relief (37:7, 36; compare a reference to the same event in 17:12–14).

The second paragraph (9–14) dwells on the failure of Jerusalem's prophets and seers to recognize the significance of the Assyrian withdrawal. They and their followers may indeed fulfill "by rote" the obligations of the cult, but "their mind has moved far from" the Lord (13). Indeed, their eyes are closed by God until in due time the prophet will be ordered "to open eyes which are shut" (compare 6:1–13 with 61:1–3).

On the other hand, to Isaiah and his disciples "the vision of the whole" (11) has been granted. Several texts illustrate that gift and the empowerment it supplies. Thus the prophetic perspective is able to penetrate past, present, and future—does not Isaiah's vision span more than two centuries and reach beyond them even into the distant past (compare 6:10–13; 7:1–9; 14:24–27, 22–23)? The vision also encompasses the wide arena of Israel's dispersion—does not Isa 1—66 address itself to those domiciled in Egypt and Mesopotamia, honoring and inviting them to pilgrims' joy? Even those who observe the Law of Moses in far-off Ethiopia and Tarshish are within the prophetic horizon (see 19:23–25; 18:7; 45:14–17; 66:18–20). Moreover, the Book of Isaiah speaks of Israel as the worldwide, peaceful vineyard of the Lord, centered in the holy mountain and its Temple in Zion (27:2–9, 12–13; compare also Introduction).

A sermon may explore the manner in which this passage invites the hearers to let themselves be led into a deeper, wider, and more fundamental understanding of the divine presence in all of creation. Blind eyes and hardened hearts are beckoned to let themselves be opened and to perceive their world with a new awareness. Those who accept this invitation will receive a fuller and more penetrating vision of life—a vision which liberates human beings from what binds or breaks them. After all, does not Moses the archprophet conclude his last words to Israel with a similar appeal (Deut 29:1–8)?

The "Woe!" over Dissenters (29:15–24)

The list of their offenses is long: secret dealings, arrogant denials, overbearing derision, deviant action, and miscarriage of justice. Who are the addressees? The identification of those wronged can more readily be made. They are the "poor among human beings," though they are worshipers of the Lord and followers of the prophetic teaching (19, 24). Moreover, the text affirms that the "blind and deaf" dissenters will hear and understand "words of a book" (18)—a notion which relates the text to the preceding one (29:1–14). There Jerusalem's prophets and seers are described as persons "in stupor," intoxicated without wine and sunk into deep sleep. Hence Isaiah's "vision of the whole" is incomprehensible to them, "like a sealed book" (9–12). The third lament, it seems, takes up the notion of a closed book which occurs in the second "woe!" passage but addresses itself more broadly to those who reject the prophet's teaching.

A sermon may focus on the notion that Israel's God is, as the all-creator, also all-knowing. Hence no human being can hide from divine scrutiny (compare Ps 139) and no group entertain the thought that it is in control of its destiny. The theme is unfolded in 40:12–26; there no fewer than five aspects of the Lord's supremacy are described. In keeping with this view, the argument for the Lord's sovereignty is repeatedly advanced through rhetorical questions which illustrate the folly of human self-sufficiency: "May the axe vaunt itself against the one who wields it?" (10:15; compare 29:16; 45:9–10). By the same token, the inescapability of the divine presence is affirmed when Israel's God is described as "the first and the last," "enthroned above the circle of the earth" (44:6; 40:22). That insight, securely held by Isaiah and his disciples, will eventually be granted to all who let the prophetic summons open their hearts (see 61:1–3; compare 42:18–44:23).

The "Woe!" over the Apostates (30:1–33)

The fourth castigation fastens on Israel as it finds itself caught between two superpowers, Assyria and Egypt. The last decades of the eighth century B.C.E. witness the gradual but relentless subjugation of Syria-Palestine by the emperors from Nineveh. The kings who held sway from Carcemish in the north to Edom and Judah in the south fought off the aggressor as well as they could, at times seeking help from the other strong nation on the scene at the time, Egypt. However, the pharaohs proved to be unreliable allies; as the Assyrian officer sent to subdue King Hezekiah of Judah put it, the monarch from the Nile is like a "splintered reed of a staff which ... punctures the palm of anyone who leans on it" (36:6).

Both the fourth and the fifth "woe!" passages (31:1—32:20) oppose those who seek Egypt's help, stressing that Israel's only hope lies in quiet trust in the Lord (30:15; 31:1–4). Moreover, both passages conclude with descriptions of divine intervention, discernible in Assyria's defeat (30:27–33; 31:8–9) and in Jerusalem's enjoyment of its former status and freedom from attack (30:19–26; 32:1–20). On the other hand, the fourth "woe!" text takes up a guideword appearing in the second and the third "woe!" passages: "a book" (compare 29:11–12 and 18). According to 30:8, its function is that of "witness for a last day." Is it the Book of Isaiah which is characterized in this manner?

The Futility of the Appeal to Egypt (30:1–7)

The reproach addresses as "apostate (literally: rebellious) sons" those who "go down to Egypt for help" without consulting the Lord. They will return red-faced because assistance will not be given to them (1–5). A short paragraph (6–7) titled "Burden of the Beasts of the Negeb" portrays in a vision pack animals making their way through the desert, loaded with gifts sent to induce Egyptian officials to accede to the Judaite request for military support.

A sermon may explore the notion of "rebellious children." The book's prologue (1:2—4:6) begins with a passage on that very theme (1:2–9) and so sets the tone for further prophetic castigation. But while that introductory text emphasizes the miracle of a remnant left by the Lord for Israel, this passage details the nature of the people's defiance. The defiance is Israel's return, of its own volition, to Egypt. Does not the Law of Moses expressly stipulate that the Lord's people, once set free from that house of bondage, must never go back (Deut 17:16)? Furthermore, are the Israelites not threatened with forced deportation to Egypt as the final and most severe punishment for disobedience (Deut 28:68)? Thus the prophet's reasoning with the Lord's wayward children is like that remonstration with a persistently defiant son which Deut 21:18–21 describes (compare also Jeremiah's similar warnings, 41:16—43:7a).

The Tablet of Witnesses (30:8–26)

Prophecies spurned are not prophecies annulled! The mouthpiece of the Lord must not abandon the divine message entrusted to him but is ordered to commit to writing what his contemporaries refused to hear. Thus it will serve in the future as witness against those who seek to silence the prophetic voice. In the first part of Isaiah also (5:1—27:13), the prophet is commanded to "seal the testimony" of his announcement of the divine rescue of the holy city from the

Syrian-Ephraimite alliance (in 734–733 B.C.E.; compare 3:23, 11–23a with 7:1—8:10). The eventual fulfillment of that promise proves that the prophet's utterance was indeed the Lord's word—is not this the standard of the Law of Moses as summarized and interpreted in Deut 1—30, which is the lawgiver's testament?

According to the same principle, in the book's second part (28:1—37:38) the prophet's rejected word is committed to writing "as witness forever." In this case, Isaiah condemns Jerusalem's pleas to Egypt for help in response to the Assyrian threat and (again!) finds his words rebuffed (compare 18:1–7 and 22:1–14). Moreover, as in the first part (compare 8:23b—9:6 with 8:11–23a), the castigation of the people's persistent reliance on human resources (15–17) is followed and balanced by the announcement of the Lord's future intervention on Jerusalem's behalf. Momentous changes are envisioned (18–26): the "visibility" of "your teacher," the profanation of the idols' silver and gold plating, the enjoyment of abundant fertility, even the sevenfold luminosity of the sun. As in other Isaianic texts, so also here the verbal images are memorable, the references to the Law of Moses important, and the horizons of the vision comprehensive.

A sermon may deal with the notion of human self-reliance. One of its biblical symbols is the horse (16; compare 31:1–3). The use of horses, especially in warfare, was associated with the exercise of power by the pharaohs of Egypt and the kings of Mesopotamia and Canaan. The humble station of Judaite kings seems only to allow the less pretentious mule as riding animal. Thus David's son Solomon rode on a mule from the Gihon Spring into the city at the occasion of his accession to the throne (1 Kings 1:33), while Zion's expected king of peace will enter Jerusalem on "an ass, a donkey foaled by a she-ass" (Zech 9:9–10; compare Mark 11:2). On the other hand, it was the same King Solomon who introduced cavalry into his army and engaged in international trade in horses and chariots (1 Kings 5:6–8 [RSV: 4:26–28]; 10:28–29); it is noteworthy that the Law of Moses expressly disapproves of that practice of Judaite kings (Deut 17:16).

Rather than relying on elaborate and frantic efforts to save themselves, the people of the Lord are urged to be quietly confident and to look in this frame of mind for divine intervention on their behalf. That kind of trust is their true strength (15)! This summons is similar to the prophet's invitation to King Ahaz a generation earlier, in which Isaiah tells the king to seek a sign from the Lord and not to rely on his own strength (7:10–17). Moreover, it is reminiscent of Moses' bidding to Israel, who finds itself pursued by Egyptian cavalry to the edge of the Red Sea: "Have no fear! Stand by and witness the deliverance which the Lord will work for you today.... The Lord will battle for you; you hold your peace!" (Exod 14:13–14). In a similar tone the following "woe!" passage (31:1—32:20) not only takes up the guideword "horse" (compare 30:16 with 31:1–3), but also affirms the sufficiency of divine intervention on Zion's behalf (31:4–5).

On the other hand, the preacher may focus on the relation of the passage to the Law of Moses, more specifically, its promulgation under King Josiah in 622 B.C.E. Several themes appear in both. There is the promise of divine mercy in response to the people's cry out of their affliction (compare 18–20a with Deut 30:1–3), but also the threat that persistent disobedience will make an army of as many as a thousand flee from the battle cry of only one attacker (compare 17 with Lev 26:7–8 and Deut 28:25). There is the announcement of the disclosure of "your teacher," whose words will enable the obedient not to deviate from the path of observance "to the right or to the left" (compare 20b–21 with Deut 28:13–14). Finally, there is the removal of the idolatrous images' covering made of precious metal such as gold (compare 22 with Deut 7:25), not to mention the description of various facets of well-being and blessing promised to those who remain loyal to the Lord (compare 23–26 with Deut 28:1–14).

The Lord's Rout of Assyria (30:27–33)

Assyria, "rod and staff of the divine anger" directed against the Lord's own people, will itself fully taste that rod (compare 31–32 with 10:5 and 15)! Indeed, a divine messenger will vanquish a large part of Sennacherib's army and in this manner liberate Jerusalem from the threat of conquest, even destruction (37:36; compare 31:8 and 10:12, 16). That victory over

Assur is announced in 27–33; it is described with images drawn from scriptural traditions which tell of comparable divine interventions. Thus the notion of "hail, thunder, and fire" as divine scourge reminds the audience of the plagues inflicted on Egypt (Exod 9:22–35), while the reference to sulphur calls to mind the destruction of Sodom and Gomorrah (Gen 19:23–25). The rainstorm motif, on the other hand, is an Isaianic metaphor for the affliction which those loyal to the Lord have to endure and from which they may shelter themselves in restored Zion (compare 4:2–6; 25:1–5; and 32:1–2).

A sermon may explore the contrast of the misery coming over Israel's attackers with the joy of those set free to feast on the Lord's holy hill (compare 29 with 27–28 and 30–33). "A night when a festival is hallowed" is the evening of Passover in the spring of the year, which ushers in the seven-day observance of the Festival of Unleavened Bread; later in the fall it is the first night of the Feast of Tabernacles (Booths) (see Lev 23:4–7 and 33–36; Num 28:16–23 and 29:12–16; and especially Lev 23:40 and Ps 122). While the first Passover night of which Scripture speaks was one marked by haste and readiness, all the following feasts of Passover and Tabernacles, observed in Jerusalem as elsewhere, are seasons of leisurely rest from pilgrim roads and enjoyment of liturgy and festive meal (compare also 52:11–12 with Exod 12:11). The Lord's deliverances of Israel from Egyptian and Assyrian (and soon also from Babylonian) oppression awaken paschal joy and so, as it were, translate the celebrants into "Eden Restored" (compare 51:1–3).

The "Woe!" over the Spirit Despisers (31:1—32:20)

The fifth "woe!" passage takes up the theme of the fourth: the people's apostasy. The divine protection of Zion against Assyria not only rules out Egyptian help, but also demands Israel's undivided loyalty to the Lord (31:1–7). The period of peace granted to Judah and Jerusalem under King Hezekiah after the Assyrians' withdrawal is celebrated (31:8–32:8), though the far-seeing eye of the prophet-visionary discerns in the pages of the future a deeply lamented ruin of "the fruitful vine" Israel; it will be brought to an end by an outpouring of divine spirit. Only then will the Lord's people find the well-being and blessing promised as the reward of loyalty (32:9–20; compare 39:1–8).

The Power of the Spirit (31:1–7)

Human sufficiency or divine intervention, flesh or spirit—this is the alternative with which those are confronted who "seek help from Egypt." To the prophet it is clear that Judah's request for assistance, directed to Pharaoh, is not only the result of failure to seek the Lord's counsel, but also the prescription for certain defeat (1–3). Jerusalem's escape from Assyrian destruction in 701 B.C.E. (see 36:1—37:38) is evidence that the Lord protects Zion as a lion defends prey torn out of the flock, even against a large number of shepherds called out to scare off the predator (4–5). The divine rescue of the city can thus lead to the invitation to the Israelites to worship in the Lord's temple; the prophet already envisions them "on that day" laying aside in contempt "gods of silver and gods of gold" (6–7).

Absence of the Spirit now, and its outpouring and presence then—this is one of the contrasts which the passage presents; note the appearance of the guideword "spirit" at its beginning and at its end (compare 31:1–3 with 32:15–20). The celestial power of the Spirit whom Israel spurns and the apparent power of the terrestrial helper to whom the nation appeals—this is another striking contrast (31:3). Thousands of besiegers threatening the holy city and the Lord's intervention comparable to a large bird hovering over its young to ward off predators—this is yet another contrast (31:4–5). Each antithesis is born of prophetic perception within its comprehensive horizons of reflection.

The rescue of Zion from the Assyrian attackers is narrated fully in 36:1—37:38; there the contrast is unfolded in vivid dialogue and focused argumentation (compare 36:4–10 with 11–12; 36:13–20 with 36:21—37:7; and 37:10–13 with 14–20/21–35). The antithesis between the current absence and the future presence of the Spirit is illustrated in Isa 1—66 by its coming to rest on one who has been set apart to announce release to the captives (61:1–3; compare 41:1–4 and 63:7–14). Finally, it is noted that the contrast of flesh with spirit is a unique notion in Isa 1—66; it will make its impact as a central motif in the theology of the Apostle Paul (Rom 8:1-9; Gal 5:16-18).

The Inauguration of Justice (31:8—32:8)

The fall of the Assyrian army through "a sword not human" brought to Hezekiah's small kingdom a period of peace and prosperity (compare 32:1-8 with 39:8b). In fact, both Isaiah and Chronicles speak of the reforms which the king carried out, specifically of his decree that sacrifices were to be offered only on the altar which was located beside the Temple in Jerusalem (see 36:7 and 2 Chron 29:1—31:21). Both passages affirm that these measures preceded the Assyrian attack. Moreover, 2 Chron 32:1-22 is at pains to point out that Zion's deliverance was the divine response to King Hezekiah's loyalty to the Lord. On the other hand, Isa 32:1-8 describes the changed situation which the royal reforms introduced: the monarch as well as his officials provide relief to all supplicants by the fair and impartial administration of justice according to the standard of Deuteronomy. Sacrilege and apostasy—in vogue under King Ahaz—give way to charitable action and exclusive loyalty to the Lord God of Israel.

The preacher notes the dramatic change which the prophet anticipates. It is reminiscent of provisions found in Deut 1—30, which—as Moses' final summary and interpretation of all other laws—was the touchstone of King Josiah's reforms and administration of justice. There is the centralization of sacrificial worship in the Temple in Jerusalem, the observance of the Passover as a pilgrimage (rather than a family) festival, and the emphasis on the importance of care for the hungry and the thirsty (presumably referring to pilgrims making their way to the holy city; see especially Deut 12:1-14; 16:1-8; and compare 28:43-48). The prophet perceives Hezekiah's actions as manifestations of obedience in these matters to the Law of Moses, a copy of which is, in accord with Deut 17:14-20, in the king's possession for his guidance. Thus Hezekiah's reign is portrayed as foretaste of that state of well-being and peace which Deut 28:1-14 promises to the obedient; and to which Isa 55:1-13 as well as 60:1-22 invite those who order their life in light of the Lord's will.

The Outpouring of Celestial Spirit (32:9–20)

Here thorn-infested field, there safe pasture; here ruined palace, there untroubled place of rest; here abject mourning, there quiet confidence—contrasts abound! Moreover, the meditative style of the visionary-prophet moves freely from an appeal to wailing women (9–14), to pleading on behalf of his community (15–19), and finally to an address directed to people who "sow by all waters" (20). Most memorable, though, is the anticipation that the (long?) period of lament over the Lord's fallen people will be ended by a "pouring out of a spirit from on high," turning "wilderness into orchard and orchard into forest," and ensuring that justice and peace reign forever (15–18).

The preacher may explore the notion of the power of the divine breath bringing about thoroughgoing change. At the beginning of the fifth "woe!" passage those who rely on earthly support, such as monies and armies brought from Egypt, are confronted by the essential distinction between the human and the divine spheres, between the terrestrial and the celestial realms, between flesh and spirit (31:1–3). The spirit whom a disloyal people disavowed will nevertheless be conveyed to them so that they overcome their self-inflicted misery. And it is the prophet who is the mediator of its tenfold work, turning dejection into rejoicing (61:1–3)!

Proceeding from the heavenly realm which it permeates and defines, the Spirit envelops the terrestrial sphere and transforms it, manifesting itself in new and unexpected ways. For instance, "wilderness turns into orchard," that is, in the lands of the dispersion those who remain (or again become) loyal to the Lord God of Israel, to the Law of Moses, and to the Temple in Jerusalem gather into congregations where holy season and cherished story of old, familiar song and inherited family rite are alive and observed; then and there fruits of the tree of life nourish, as it were, the faithful once again (compare 27:2–9; 43:16–21; and Joel 3:1–2 [RSV: 2:28–29]). Does not the outpouring of the Spirit on Jesus' disciples, witnessed by pilgrims assembled in Jerusalem from all the regions of the Jewish diaspora in the Roman-Hellenistic world (Acts 2:1–42), attest to that very spiritual renewal?

The "Woe!" over the Ravager (33:1-9)

The last "woe!" text is the most cryptic, at least in its reference to the ravager (1). Who is he? Not only do nations and peoples scatter when he appears, but four regions of northern and central Palestine (Lebanon, Sharon, Carmel, and Bashan) are laid waste by him (3, 9). Readers cannot but think of Assyria, aptly characterized in this fashion. Furthermore, the guideword of the opening line ("ravager") has already appeared in 16:4 with reference to the armies from Nineveh, and in 21:2 that very word is coupled (in inverted order) with the second guideword "deceiver." The text contrasts that superpower, which fills the world to overflow, with the Lord's reassuring presence "on high" and the divine gift of "justice and right" to Zion (5). Thus the following verse can duly emphasize that this knowledge is Israel's treasure (6; compare 11:2), and the earlier plea for divine intervention (vs. 2) can anticipate that assurance.

A sermon may explore the difference between divine and human perspectives. According to the latter, superpowers dominate, claiming all attention and exhausting the will to resist. The divine perspective, on the other hand, offers the longer, the wider, and the deeper view. Radical reversals may change all constellations, and that quickly and completely (compare 9:4-5 and 24:1-2; also 1 Sam 2:1-10). It was such a radical reversal that freed Jerusalem from the Assyrian threat overnight (see 36:1—37:38)!

The Invitation to the City of Assembly (33:10-35:10)

The six "woe!" texts in 28:1—33:9 are followed in 33:10—35:10 by a text cluster which celebrates "Zion, the city of our assemblies" (33:20). First, the requirements made of those who come to worship on the holy hill, whether they come from across the seas or merely from a town close to Jerusalem, are laid out (33:10-16), then a vision of Zion's rise to eminence and of its enduring existence (33:17-24) is put against the dark foil of the disappearance of Edom, one of its competitors (34:1-17). Finally, the new life of faith made possible for those whose eyes have been opened (35:1-10) is described.

Qualifications for Welcome in Zion (33:10–16)

The transition from the sixth "woe!" text (33:1–9) to the list of ethical requirements laid upon the Lord's faithful (33:13–16) is fluid; 33:10–12 can also be connected to what precedes. These verses are in fact a hinge which identifies Jerusalem's rise, against the backdrop of the nations' woes, as the work of "the Lord's rising" (10). The Lord's announcement of his imminent intervention to quell opposition introduces the call to "the far and the near" to recognize his activity for what it is. The addressees are the members of the worldwide community of Judaism, here divided into those who live in dispersion, whether in Galilee or across the seas, and those who live in and near Jerusalem. In 57:19 (56:9—57:21) the opposition "far–near" also appears; there it describes the gift of divine blessing which unites not only proselyte and born Israelite or Judaite, but also settlers and pilgrims, with those who are residents of the land of promise from times of old.

A sermon may deal with the blessing through which unity in religious observance is able to bridge differences of birth, station in life, and mother tongue. But it may also focus on the qualifications for welcome into that community of loyalty to the Lord. The ethics of the faithful can be simply summarized, as here, in no more than six commandments (33:15). Not surprisingly, "walking in righteousness" as the basic qualification begins the series and points to a known and accepted standard of behavior (compare Deut 16:18–20). The preacher notes similar lists of simple requirements found in Pss 15 and 24. They all deal with interhuman relationships by setting up easily remembered and practiced demands, comparable to the second part of the "Ten Words" (or "Commandments"; Exod 20:7–14; Deut 5:11–18). Moreover, the lack of lengthy, numerous, or detailed lists of regulations underscores in its own way the importance of broad guidelines and of living in the spirit of loyalty.

Zion's and Edom's Futures (33:17—32:17)

A study in contrasts indeed! Here Zion's exaltation, there Edom's demise! Here eternal safety, there everlasting chaos! Here a whole and well-ordered world where even sickness is no more, there devastated ruins in which demons roam! The old and deep tension between Edom and Judah (Jer 49:7–22; Ezek 25:12–14; Amos 1:11–12; Obad), between Esau and Jacob (Gen 25:20–33; 27:1–45; 32:5—33:17), is the scriptural setting against which the passage must be read (compare also 64:1–6). Readers also call to mind that "Edom" not only is the proper name of one of Israel's and Judah's sister nations, but can shade over into a cover name for whoever is at a given time the great adversary of the people of the Lord. Thus when Rome was the enemy, its name was—Edom!

The Vision of Zion's Endurance (33:17–24)

Few texts in Isa 1—66 are as exuberant as this one. Words of acclamation and praise almost tumble over each other, eager to lift high "Zion, the city of our assemblies" and "the Lord (as) judge and lawgiver, king and savior" together. Equally strong are the negations: a poetic (and rare) particle of negation ("not") occurs no fewer than seven times! It is used to deny emphatically that Jerusalem shall ever again be forced to pull up stakes and be exiled (20) or "foreign ships sail its waters," that is, that the city will have to endure conquests again (21), or that there will ever be people within its walls who have to admit that they are sick (24)!

The preacher may wish to explore the notion of the Lord's kingship (see especially 17 and 24). The passage presents a veritable catalogue of divine attributes: the Lord God of Israel is enthroned in beauty and sovereignty, exercising the offices of judge and lawgiver, protecting the holy city completely and forever, celebrated as king and most of all as the one who intervenes on behalf of his people. Readers of Isaiah know that the Lord's kingship is witnessed by prophets called into the heavenly court (see 6:1–13, and compare Jer 23:15–24 and 1 Kings 22:19–23). These texts show that the prophets made privy to the celestial council are sent to convey the Lord's own words to their contemporaries—more often than not finding their message spurned and themselves set aside.

On the other hand, readers knowledgeable in the Scriptures also know that the claim of the Lord's kingship is primarily directed to the gods of the other nations who can and do tempt Israelites and Judaites to worship them and thus to become apostates (note the example of King Solomon, 1 Kings 11:1–8). Ps 82 allows us a glimpse into the theological struggle which leads to the (theological) affirmation of the supremacy of the God of Israel: judged by the humanitarian standards of Israel's law, other gods fall short; therefore they lose their divine status and are demoted to human positions! Thus the first commandment of the "Ten Words" appropriately prohibits Israel from worshiping any god "before" Israel's deity, that is, placing it higher than the Lord (Exod 20:3; Deut 5:7). In keeping with this view the Song of the Sea (Exod 15:1–18) asks, "Who is like you, O Lord, among the gods?" (11) and concludes with the clear and short affirmation, "The Lord will reign (as king) for ever and ever." In the words of Isaiah speaking on behalf of Israel's God, "I am the Lord, your Holy One, the creator of Israel, your king" (43:15; compare 44:6 and 52:7).

A sermon may also deal with the notion of "Jerusalem as the city of assembly." Is not Mount Zion with its Temple the center of the world of Judaism? Is it not the hope of every observant member of the Lord's people to stand one day "within your gates, O Jerusalem" (Ps 122:2)? Are not pilgrimages to the Temple a well-known and gladly accepted custom in Judaism still today? After all, according to Moses' farewell speech (Deuteronomy) and the (Deuteronomistic) narrator of 1 Kings, the map of Israel's and Judah's sacred geography is a series of concentric circles centered in the Temple and the altar placed next to it (note the role of the newly dedicated Temple as the focus of Israel's world in 1 Kings 8:22–61, and the relation of Israelites wherever they may find themselves in the ancient world to the Temple, as assumed in "Blessings and Curses" in Deut 28—29).

Moreover, it is Deuteronomy's Moses who decrees that the three annual festivals (Passover/Unleavened Bread—Pentecost—Tabernacles) be observed, not in the traditional manner as family feasts, but as pilgrimages which bring all the faithful to the one, holy city (Deut 16), where they are invited to celebrate together in gladness (see Deut 12:2–7 and Ps 122). At these occasions the ties of tribe and friendship are renewed, the worldwide community of Israel reaffirmed, and shared memory turned into assurance for the present and hope for the future. Luke's story of the pilgrimage of Jesus' family (2:41-51) illustrates this, as do the words of the Jewish historian Josephus, who lived in the first century of our era. He specifically mentions the pilgrims' joint thanksgivings and supplications, the nurture of their mutual affections, and hence the forestalling of their becoming absolute strangers to each other (*Antiquities* IV 203-4).

The Announcement of Edom's Disappearance (34:1-17)

This countertext to the preceding and following passages (33:17-24 and 35:1-10) is as strongly negative in its description of the nations' and specifically Edom's fall as the framing texts are positive in their verbal imagery. Its first four verses (34:1-4) announce the Lord's defeat of the peoples of the world, of their armies, and their heavenly hosts; like falling leaves in the autumn they will come to nothing. It is the same theme as that of the second section (13-27) of the book's first part (5-27), but there it is much more fully and broadly developed. However, Edom is not included there—was it left out in order to provide the sinister background here for the radiance of Zion's restoration?

The preacher notes the varied imagery in the description of Edom's fall: that of war (5), sacrificial ritual (6-7), legal procedure (8), ancient lore such as the fiery pitch and sulphur of Sodom's and Gomorrah's destruction (9; compare Gen 19:23), not to mention the ominous use of the word pair "void and empty" which, very rare in Scripture, describes the unordered, still chaotic condition which obtained before creation (11; compare Gen 1:2).

Thus a sermon may deal with the—for us—troubling manner in which in certain passages of Scripture the opponents of the Lord and of Israel are pictured as condemned to eternal destruction, their fate described in warlike, violent words. We note that then (as still today) warlike and violent actions were everyday experiences which narrators, poets, and lawgivers sought to comprehend. Many came to understand them as divine interventions, whether for good or for bad. This is illustrated by Amos' question, "Can misfortune come to a town, if the Lord has not caused it?" (3:6b) and by the divine assertion in Isa 45:7, "I make weal and I make woe—I the Lord do all these things."

The reflection of prophetic authors such as Isaiah and Jeremiah moves beyond this insight to the certainty that even the powerful armies of Assyria and Babylonia are nothing but the rod of the Lord's anger (see Isa 10:5 and Jer 25:3–11). Small wonder that poetic and narrative conceptualizations of the Lord's future intervention also employ the warlike imagery which other authors, then as well as now, replace with tolerant and reconciling modes of expression. In short, exclusive and particularistic ways of speaking are already in Scripture held in check, if not overcome, by inclusive and universalistic ways of thinking and feeling. For Isaiah's emphasis see the hope expressed in 19:18–25 that one day Egypt and Assyria shall together with Israel be called "peoples of the Lord."

Eye Opening on the Holy Road (35:1–10)

The wonders of the new exodus exceed by far those of the Exodus from Egypt! Moses' Israel, shielded and led by the divine presence, had nevertheless to face a roadless desert (Exod 13:20–22). Now the redeemed of the Lord find their way prepared and ready! Then the wilderness inspired dread and the desire to return to the meat pots of the valley of the Nile (Deut 1:19; Exod 16:2–3). Now nothing, certainly no wild animals, need be feared by the wayfarers! Then the Lord's people had to endure thirst which led them almost into rebellion (Exod 15:22–25). Now springs, even streams of water, appear at the sojourners' feet! Then the spies' report disheartened the Israelites to the point of disobedience and the desire to murder Moses (Num 13—14). Now weak hands and feet are strengthened for the march! In short, here as in 43:8–21, themes and imagery of the stories of the Exodus of old provide base and foil so that 35:1–10 can depict the (re-)turn of the Lord's faithful to Zion as a greater exodus still.

A sermon may fasten on the bold notion that blind people will be able to see, deaf to hear, lame to jump, and mute to speak (5–6a; compare 32:3–4). The text is indeed warrant for the assurance that the liberation of the handicapped is nothing but a clear example of the divine will to set persons free from what constrains them. Appropriate as such interpretation of the passage is, a look at Deut 29:3 (1-8) suggests a still more far-reaching interpretation. There Moses says in the concluding part of his farewell speech that even after the marvels of the Exodus from Egypt and the severe test of forty years of wandering in the wilderness, Israel has "not (yet) been given a mind to understand or eyes to see or ears to hear."

In other words, what the first exodus did not and could not accomplish has now, during a greater exodus still, become reality. It is nothing less than a spiritual awakening which the prophet perceives happening on "the holy road," whenever persons set out on journeys of faith, the goal of which is the place of divine presence. Thus Isaiah's announcement of such internalization of Israel's sacred legacy, in the process of realizing itself under the impact of prophetic words of challenge and promise, corresponds to Jeremiah's and Deuteronomy's call for a circumcision of the heart (Deut 10:12-22; Jer 4:1-4). Early Jewish and Christian literature provides further examples of renewed, spiritual appropriations of the scriptural heritage (compare the quotation of Isa 35:5 by the Gospel of Mark in order to show that in Jesus' restoration of the deaf-mute person [7:30-37] divine power is also at work).

Narrative Review of Sennacherib's Humiliation (36:1—37:38)

Isaiah 36—37/38—39 as Conceptual Link and Literary Hinge

The sustained narration Isa 36—39 has claimed our attention in the Introduction. There a double thesis is presented: (1) Its word-for-word correspondence to 2 Kings 18:13, 17—20:19 makes Isa 1—66 a part of the larger work to which 2 Kings also belongs. That work is the encyclopedic composition usually called "The Law and the Prophets" (see the discussion in the Introduction). Also note that 2 Chron 32:1-24 partially corresponds to 2 Kings 18:13—20:19, but since the former is part of a literarily separate work, this correspondence is not further discussed here. (2) The first of the two parts of Isa 36—39, that is, 36:1—37:38, presents in a patterned, exemplary fashion that fivefold motif sequence which is characteristic of the entire book's thematic structure, both in its larger and in many of its smaller text units (see the discussion of "Thematic Structure"). In short, the motif series moves from (1) extreme threat to (2) submissive appeal, followed by (3) divine assurance, (4) celebration, and (5) statement of divine rescue.

Here we note that the first text unit (36:1—37:38) looks back on the humiliation of the Assyrian emperor Sennacherib and on Jerusalem's escape from conquest by his army. On the other hand, the second text unit (38:1—39:8) is loosely connected to the first in that it places its narration of Hezekiah's illness, recovery, and response to the Babylonian embassy expressing sympathy "in those days" (38:1), that is, in the days of the Assyrian threat. Hence review is followed by preview; the whole of 36—39 looks both backward and forward, both to the past and to the future.

The double function of the narrative identifies it as a conceptual link between the second and the third part of the book, connecting the past humiliation of the Assyrians to the anticipated humiliation of the Babylonians. The escape of Jerusalem from the former threat makes manifest the pattern of divine intervention for days to come, notably for the more deadly threat which the Babylonian destruction of city, Temple, and palace in 587 B.C.E. presents. Thus 36:1—37:38 is here discussed as a closing review of the book's second part, and 38:1—39:8 as an opening preview and stage setting for its third part (38:1/40:1—55:13). In short, the narration is the literary hinge which aligns Israel's escape from Babylon with that from Nineveh several generations before.

Historical Background

In the "Sennacherib Prism," now in the Oriental Institute of the University of Chicago, that king boasts that he has made "Hezekiah, the Judaite, . . . a prisoner in Jerusalem, his royal residence, like a bird in a cage." He claims to have conquered forty-six fortified cities and taken 200,100 prisoners but does not say that he has captured Hezekiah's city. This information agrees with the biblical text, as does the other, that he increased the tribute he required the Judaite monarch to pay (see 2 Kings 18:14-18, but not mentioned in Isa 36) after "the terror-inspiring splendor of my lordship had overwhelmed" him.

It is to these events that Isa 36—37 and 2 Kings 18—19 (as well as 2 Chron 32) directly, and Isa 28-35 and 14:24-28 indirectly, refer. The escape of the city from seemingly certain conquest is portrayed by the prophet not as human accomplishment but as the work of the Lord God of Israel (37:5-7, 26-29, 36 = 2 Kings 19:5-7, 25, 28, 35). The Introduction shows how this notion is juxtaposed to Jerusalem's escape from a similar fate a generation earlier and, by the same token, anticipates a corresponding rescue of the holy city from the Babylonians.

The Double Challenge of 36:1—37:38

Readers quickly note that Hezekiah and his people must twice endure the verbal attacks of the Assyrians: first the Rabshakeh, an officer sent by "the great king" (36:4), addresses Hezekiah's officials as well as the defenders on Jerusalem's walls without, however, receiving a direct answer (36:1—37:9a). Then Assyrian messengers arrive with a letter from Sennacherib; it presents a still starker challenge. Again, the answer is not immediately forthcoming but is eventually given when "the Lord's angel" strikes the Assyrian camp while the king, having returned to Nineveh, is assassinated (37:9b-38; compare 7).

The Futility of the Rabshakeh's Challenge (36:1—37:9a)

As elsewhere in many biblical narratives, the argument is carried by dialogues. This enables the audience to concentrate on the words exchanged and to follow their interaction as they seek to inform and to probe, to accuse or to challenge, to sow suspicion or to convince. Here the formulations are clear, direct, and graphic (note for instance the reference to Egypt's help as "the broken reed of a staff, which will pierce the hand of any one who leans on it," 36:6; also 12 and 17). Moreover, unusual shifts in literary execution appear, such as a strategic move from one language to another (36:11-12), a psychologically convincing shift from dissuasion to persuasion (36:13–20), and a contrast between pleading and its reception in silence (36:13–20/21). In short, the reflective mode captures the severity of the challenge as well as the fearful yet considered response by Hezekiah and his officers.

The preacher notes that both speeches of the Assyrian emissary (36:4–10 and 13–20) are catalogues of arguments one might bring forward against the thesis that the Lord, the God of Israel, is supreme over other deities and in sovereign command of all that happens on earth. These are actually tenets held by "A Book of Remembrance" in general and Isa 1—66 in particular. The three arguments of the first speech show that Egypt is worse than no help at all, that Hezekiah cannot count on the support of his God since he has reduced his worship to only one altar, and that the Judaite king would not even have enough horsemen should the Assyrians supply him with 2,000 horses. One senses a note of triumph as the Rabshakeh clinches the argument with the assertion that it is actually the God of Israel who has sent the Assyrians against Jerusalem—quite in keeping with Isaiah's assertion that Assyria is "the rod of the Lord's anger" (10:5)!

The second set of arguments dismisses Judah's leaders and addresses itself to the defenders who witness the proceedings from the city's walls. They are pointedly addressed in their own Judaite language—the Assyrian officer had refused the request to negotiate in the Aramaic tongue, which Hezekiah's officials profess to know. Now the warning against reliance on Hezekiah and on his equally powerless God gives way to a plea to the men on the wall, who are desperately hungry and thirsty, to let themselves be resettled in Assyria, a land as fertile, fruitful, and hospitable as their own.

A sermon may trace the intriguing exchanges between the challengers and the challenged. Against the many words and the logical arguments which are put forth, the city's defenders observe silence, knowing that it is not in their power to give the answer. If there is an answer, it is their divine Lord who must supply it! All they can do is to turn to Isaiah, the prophet, who may intercede on their behalf. This is indeed the theme of the last text unit of the passage (36:22—37:9a).

The officers' and the king's first response is a gesture of mourning: they tear their garments. Then the officials as well as the senior priests are sent by Hezekiah to Isaiah with the request for intercession in response to the "blasphemy." The divine answer through the prophet is brief but reassuring: Sennacherib will withdraw and eventually be assassinated in his own land.

A sermon may deal with the manner in which the narrative portrays trust in the Lord. It is the first response to a trying situation and precludes relying on one's own resources. Trust in the Lord is shown by king as well as priest, by official as well as commoner. Such trust turns to the prophet as the one who mediates the divine will (compare Num 12:6–8; also 1 Sam 28:6). Submission to the Lord's action, as it manifests itself in the plight in which the supplicants find themselves, is expressed in words of sorrow and appeal. Fittingly, the narrative calls for the quiet confidence which the book contrasts elsewhere with the people's desire to rely on their own strength (compare 30:15–17 and 7:10–17).

The End of Sennacherib's Blasphemy (37:9b–38)

The second set of exchanges, narratively framed like the first one, presents the Assyrian emperor himself as he utters words of challenge, nay, blasphemy to Hezekiah. Spurred by the news of the advance of the Cushite King Tirhaka, Sennacherib seeks to persuade the Judaite king with the argument that his God is as powerless as the gods of the kings whose cities have already fallen into Assyrian hands (9b–13). In response, Hezekiah "spreads the letter (scroll) out before the Lord" in the Temple. He pleads that the Lord rescue them, since the God of Israel alone is truly God. But he also acknowledges that the Assyrian claims based on their conquests cannot be ignored (14–20).

The answer is given through Isaiah in a poem of considerable length (21–35). It begins with a ridicule of Assyrian arrogance which is in part reminiscent of the manner in which the residents of the underworld detail the acts of vainglory of the Babylonian king when he descends to the shadows after his final defeat (compare 22–25 with 14:4–20). The passage then comes quickly to an end with the narration of the Assyrians' loss of their camp, the king's return to Nineveh, and his assassination there (37:36–38).

The preacher notes not only the condemnation of arrogance (29), but also the affirmation of the Lord's supremacy. From of old the God of Israel has planned the actions of human rulers and thus knows all their moves (compare 26, 28; also 45:1–7). Furthermore, what the Lord does and will do is vindicated for the prophet's audience through signs, which are given now as they were given in the past and will be given in the future (compare 30–32 with 7:10–17 and 38:7–8); do not the prophet and his disciples constitute a chain of "signs and portents in Israel" (8:16–18; 20:1–6; 50:4–9; 61:1–3)?

Finally, the certainty of the divine protection of the holy city "for the Lord's and for David's sake" (35) fits into the perspective of the book, whose central theme is the transformation of Zion from deserted hut to honored center of worldwide Judaism. Here if anywhere the preacher recognizes the promise as well as the liability of a piety which assures itself of a center located in space—tangible token of an encounter with the divine. Zion and its Temple emerged as such and ordered the world of Judaism around Jerusalem (see Dan 6:11; Luke 2:41–51; John 12:20; Acts 2:5–11). Similarly, Islamic piety turns to Mecca as place of pilgrimage, and Christian devotion has through the centuries come to honor not only Jerusalem, Nazareth, and Bethlehem, but also Rome and Byzantium as centers of its communions, not to mention special places more recently identified. However, the faithful also know that the divine presence is ultimately free and unbound (comp. Isa 66:1–4; John 3:8). It creates community wherever human beings, many or few, gather in devotion and study—so both the Evangelist Matthew and Rabbi Chananya, son of Teradyon, affirm (Matt 18:29; Pirqe Aboth 3:3).

PART 3
THE VISION OF BABYLON'S FALL AND ZION'S RESTORATION
(Isaiah 38:1—55:13)

The narration of Isa 36—39 not only connects the book to its larger literary context, but also presents by way of example the thematic motif sequence which is the characteristic feature of Isa 1—66. Moreover, the introductory discussion of 36:1—37:38 above shows that its sequel, the stories of Hezekiah's miraculous recovery and his response to the Babylonian embassy (38:1–39:8), provides the glimpse into the future which the next part of the book demands. Thus with 38:1—39:8 the stage is set for the presentation of the prophet's vision of the future: the mission of the Lord's servant (40:1—55:13). Its first segment (40:1—47:15) enlightens the people called Jacob-Israel so that it may perceive what the Lord is doing in its midst (43:19). The second segment (48:1—55:13) expands the mission and invites Abraham and Sarah's kin to share in the re-creation of Jacob-Israel (51:1—2). Thus, the book's third part affirms and transcends the preceding ones in that the two deliverances of Jerusalem of which they tell (733 and 701 B.C.E.) provide warrant and paradigm for the Lord's greater intervention: the rebuilding of Zion as the center for all who honor her as "their mother" (49:14–21; 54:1–3).

Narrative Preview of Judah's Exile to Babylon (38:1—39:8)

Two units make up the section. The first is the narrative of Hezekiah's mortal illness and miraculous recovery (38:1–22); the second, the story of the monarch's friendly reception of a Babylonian embassy and of an ominous prophecy by Isaiah in response (39:1–8). The first provides not only the setting for "The Poem of Hezekiah" (38:9–20), but also the occasion for the plot of the second.

Hezekiah's Miraculous Recovery (38:1–22)

The story shows how Hezekiah also acts in his personal life in accord with the pattern which the book lays out for the faithful: the prophet's announcement of certain death is accepted in humility, but also with a plea for divine intervention. This is indeed granted and leads to the supplicant's grateful acknowledgment of the heaven-sent rescue. The unit presents this paradigm in the form of both prose and poetry (compare 1–8, 21–22, with 9–20).

The poem of Hezekiah is not paralleled in 2 Kings—an indication, it seems, that "The Law and the Prophets" as the more comprehensive work leaves to the prophetic book the exploration of the internal thoughts and emotions of a major figure. Thus the poem, spoken by the king in the first person singular, retraces first his despair over the untimely death which the prophet has announced (10–15) and then his surprise at the divine change of mind, evidently in response to his earnest prayer (16–17), and concludes with a vow of future public thanksgiving for deliverance (18–20).

A sermon may deal with the pain of coping with the certainty of terminal illness. The poem takes it seriously and acknowledges the depression and the questioning which accompany it. Only when this is done is it possible to move beyond it—whether or not a hoped-for reprieve is granted. Given the orientation of 38:1–39:8 toward the future (and the following story shows that it is the Babylonian exile which is in view), one wonders whether the poem of Hezekiah might anticipate a divine reprieve when destruction and exile seem to spell only doom and death. Does not King Solomon's Temple dedication prayer already affirm that even defeat and deportation will not be able to separate the supplicants from divine intervention on their behalf (1 Kings 8:33–34, 46–53)?

On the other hand, the preacher may deal with Hezekiah's assertion that the Lord has put the king's "sins" out of sight, behind God's back (17). This formulation is one of many in Scripture which refer to divine forgiveness, that is, God's willingness to overcome whatever separates human beings from the divine presence. For many people the notion of sin is primarily a moral one, that is, concerned with actions against the second table of "The Ten Commandments." However, the biblical notion of sin is first of all related to the first table, to turning away from or not seeking the divine presence as it is found in sacred rite and holy place, in festive season or inherited Scripture, in religious community or personal meditation. Hence the terms "apostasy" and "idolatry" suggest themselves as more fitting translations of that biblical word. Hezekiah's poem illustrates that whenever human beings find themselves separated from the divine presence, we are called to respond with the acknowledgment of that separation, in whatever way it may have come about. Hence, the king can speak of his "sins" even though he is portrayed—and portrays himself—as exemplary in his loyalty to the Lord (37:1–5, 14–20; 38:2–3)! In sum, the biblical notion of "sin" as separation from the divine presence identifies its basic element and suggests that concrete transgressions of the commandments are manifestations of one's distance from God. The psalmist thus can affirm that "for me it is good to be near God" (Ps 73:28).

The Announcement of Judah's Future Exile to Babylon (39:1–8)

This brief narrative is of great importance because it relates the future fate of Judah as implied in the book's third part (38:1—55:13) to the two deliverances of the holy city as told in its first and second parts (5:1—27:13; 28:1—37:38).

Hezekiah has welcomed a Babylonian royal embassy congratulating him after his recovery and has shown the visitors from afar all the treasures of his kingdom (1–2). When Isaiah inquires and is told what has transpired (3–4), he relays the Lord's word of a future transportation of all Judaite royal treasures and of male descendants of Hezekiah to Babylon (5–7). The king however, seems to shrug off the announcement as not affecting his own reign (8).

Readers cannot but note this anticipation, for the first time spoken clearly. To be sure, Babylon's demise has already been described in narrative detail and poetic imagery (13:1—14:23). Now it seems that Babylon's fall will be preceded by

Judah's, distant though it may appear in the vision of a prophet speaking more than a century before it will occur. Here the audience perceives the wide horizons of time and space within which the prophet comprehends events spanning several generations and great distances.

In other words, the deep break in the people's history, represented by the destruction of Jerusalem and the deportation of its leading circles by the Babylonian king Nebuchadnezzar in 587 B.C.E., is within the prophetic—and the prophet's—purview. Now the stage is set for the divine words which appoint Jacob-Israel as the Lord's servant people and give it a new mission. Now the audience is ready for the consoling and probing, pleading and reassuring poems of 40:1—55:13.

Release Into a New Creation (40:1—55:13)

Soaring word and humbling reproach, patient argument and urgent call, intimate reflection and public invitation—the poetry of Isa 40–55 is sure to capture its audience. While passages similar in style and theme appear elsewhere in the book (compare 12:1–6; 35:1–10; 60:1–22), this sustained sequence of longer and shorter units paints a comprehensive picture of Jacob-Israel's rise to new life, made possible by Babylon's fall and Cyrus' edict (see 2 Chron 36:22–23; compare 13:1—14:23; 43:14–15; 52:11–12).

The verbal imagery is varied: motifs from the spheres of nature and creation, of the patriarchs and the Exodus from Egypt, of cultic ritual and idolatrous practice are evoked in the service of consolation, reflection, and persuasion. The prophet's words address Jacob-Israel, the remnant people, and seek to open its eyes to the new which the Lord is doing in its midst. That humble group is appointed as the Lord's servant and charged to call all Israel into the divine presence. However, the ultimate goal is still higher: Jacob-Israel's mission is not limited to Jacob's descendants; he is to become "a light to the nations" (49:6), that is, the instrument of the divine restoration of creation at large.

The climactic nature of the section is evident in its two segments: the first (40:1—47:15) portrays the remnant's appointment as servant sent to Israel at large, and the second (48:1—

55:13), the expansion of that mission. Both begin with affirmations of the Lord's interventions (40:1–31; 48:1–22), proceed to present the servant's mandates (41:1–42:17; 49:1—50:11), and then describe aspects of the divine recreation, portraying its promise (42:18—44:23; 44:24—46:13/ 51:1—52:6; 54:1—55:13) as well as its pain (47:1–15/52:7—53:12).

The Mission of the Servant (40:1—47:15)

The divine intervention, based on the Lord's supremacy in creation and the encouragement of Israel (40:1–31), sets the stage for Jacob-Israel's appointment as the Lord's servant (41:1—42:17). Five gifts of insight are given him (42:18—44:23), so that he may claim the new life made possible through Jerusalem's restoration and the ingathering of its children (44:24—46:13). Babylon, however, the erstwhile despot, must humble itself (47:1–15). The second segment (48:1—55:13) describes still greater tasks for the servant (49:1—50:11) but also speaks of the extreme suffering his mission will bring him (52:7—53:12).

The Consolation of Jacob-Israel (40:1–31)

The images are memorable and the horizon is wide: here stands humbled Zion awaiting the turn of its fate, there is the Lord enthroned above the earth's circle; here is the desert track turned level road, there the shepherd tending ewes and lambs; here is despair-ridden Jacob, there the eagle ready to soar. The addressee of the prophet-visionary's words is Jacob-Israel (1–2, 3–5, 27–31) or Jerusalem, either directly (9–11) or indirectly (1–2). Both are comforted and encouraged as the text moves from the announcement of the divine intervention liberating the captives (1–11) to the fourfold argument for the Lord's supremacy (12–26) and concludes with words of encouragement (27–31).

The Divine Intervention (40:1–11)

The prophet urgently commands Israel, the remnant people, to console the people of Israel at large. Thus at the very beginning of the segment the task given to Israel is in view (compare 42:1–4 and 49:1–6). Since Jerusalem is, figuratively speaking, Israel's mother (49:14–21; 54:1–4), the city is the first one to be assured of the end of her misery. Soon the prophet will proclaim outright that it will be rebuilt and become a larger, more prosperous city than before (44:28; compare 60:1–22).

The preacher notes that Zion's future is as the tangible, spiritual center of the Lord's people wherever they find themselves, whether returnees or pilgrims. Now is heard the call of "a voice" from the celestial sphere. But while the prophet originally heard a heavenly order to close his people's ears to the divine voice (6:1–13), he now speaks to persons who have already endured the double devastation and exile of which the earlier command had spoken. The time has come for the people to witness the divine glory present in the Temple (3–5; compare Exod 40:34–35; 1 Kings 8:10–11). Does not the Persians' tolerance, as well as their network of imperial highways, encourage journeys "home" (compare 2 Chron 36:22–23)?

A sermon may explore the second celestial call which the prophet is privileged to hear: it affirms the validity of the Lord's word, once spoken, for generations to come, thus outlasting the seasonal growth and decay of nature (6–8). Has the word not been sealed in the prophet and his disciples, awaiting its realization until two destructions and exiles pass over land and people (8:16–18; 6:11–13)? Small wonder that other speakers have affirmed powerfully that the word of the Lord is the enduring medium of revelation (see Jer 23:23–29; Amos 3:7; compare Isa 55:10–11).

Finally, the preacher notes that the city is commanded to act as herald of the good news of a new beginning for "the cities of Judah" (9–11). This passage calls to mind a similar one according to which the returnees and pilgrims become "heralds of peace" for Jerusalem (52:7–10). Their call finds its climax in the affirmation that "the Lord reigns as king" (55:7; compare Exod 15:18). In both passages the prophet speaks of "the good news," employing the word which in early Christian writings is the term for the proclamation of the renewed offer of life to the Lord's people which Jesus' word and work enact (Mark 1:14–15; Rom 1:16–17).

The Lord's Supremacy (40:12–26)
Rhetorical questions, phrased positively (12, 13, 18, 25, 26) as well as negatively (21), set the tone for this meditative discourse on the Lord's transcendence beyond all that human beings are able to comprehend. The prophet argues, as it were, with an audience (or within himself), moving through four related, though different, aspects of divine sovereignty.

There is (1) the Lord's order of the visible universe which transcends the grasp of mortals (12–14). Then (2) there is the divine greatness, making "the nations" who seem to loom large nothing but "specks of dust on weighing scales," that is, of no real account (15–17). Further, (3) the prophet deals with human-made images to which the Lord, creator of all, cannot be compared (18–24). Finally, there is (4) the witness of the ordered heavenly host, each called by name and completing its appointed task (25–26).

Any one of these aspects may be developed in a sermon on the sovereignty of the God of Israel. While philosophers speak (like Isa 40:12–14) with admiration and awe of the immensity and the rhythms of the universe, one of the creation stories (Gen 1:2—2:4a) undertakes to describe the coming into being of the terrestrial realm as marked by order and measure which human beings may retrace and make manifest. Another theme is that of dimensions and proportions (15–17): what in human perception fills all of space and time is in divine perspective of little account. Biblical writers have also reflected on that topic in relation to the passing of ages (compare 2 Peter 3:8 with Ps 90:4).

Finally, a sermon may deal with the Lord's incomparability (18–24). Here the subject is related to that of idolatry. Already the brief summary of Israel's obligations, the Ten Commandments, impresses on the faithful that they must not fashion a likeness of the God of Israel (Exod 20:4–6; Deut 5:8–10). Repeatedly, Israel's failure to keep this commandment is condemned (Exod 32:1–8; Num 25:1–9; Judg 2:6–23; 17:1–6; 1 Kings 11:1–8) and the impotence of idols maintained (40:19–20; 41:6–7; 44:9–20; compare Jer 10:1–16). This text reaches further: the rise and fall of powerful rulers, witnessed by the remnant people more than once within memory, is interpreted as the Lord's work, "lest Israel claim, 'My idol has done this'" (48:5). The words given to the prophet are still more explicit: "I form light and create darkness, I make weal and create woe ..." (45:7). Statements like these introduce the subject of "theodicy," that is, the attempt to explain the presence of evil in a world where God alone is considered supreme and cause of all that happens. Such discussion must also reflect on God's seeming acquiescence in innocent suffering and its effects on the afflicted (compare Ps 73 and Job 33:12–30).

Empowerment of Weary Israel (40:27–31)

As usual in this part of the book, Jacob-Israel is addressed. Readers recognize that the double name is suggested by one of the memorable stories found in "The Law": Jacob's struggle with the angel (Gen 32:22–32). From it the patriarch emerged not only limping but also with a new name, given to him by the powerful but nameless "man" after Jacob's victory. "Israel" will be Jacob's name, "because you have striven with God and with men, and have prevailed" (28). This change gives the patriarch the name under which the twelve tribes descended from him (and in due time the kingdom comprising all of them but Judah) appear in the Hebrew Scriptures, and which remained important for NT writings (Matt 2:6; Luke 7:9; John 1:31; Rom 9:6). Thus, the double name identifies the people of the Lord through their ancestor, both as physically descended from that patriarch and as spiritually tested and readied for their mission (compare 43:1–7 and 44:21–22).

On the other hand, a sermon may deal with the text's guideword, "weary." It appears four times, twice each as noun and as verb. It aptly describes the state in which the remnant people finds itself, and that in marked contrast to the divine strength which is offered. The brief passage has become for many "who wait for the Lord," whatever their station in life, a cherished word of consolation. The comparison between those empowered and "eagles whose wings are ready to lift" fittingly concludes the text.

The Appointment of the Servant (41:1—42:17)

Three smaller units follow each other, highlighting different aspects of the servant's mission. The first (41:1–20) identifies the servant by addressing Jacob-Israel (see 8–9), the second (41:12—42:4) introduces him to the audience (see 42:1), and the third (42:5–17) defines his mission (see 6–7). Thus, the servant motif provides the major focus. Moreover, each of the smaller units is made up of paragraphs which deal with aspects of the main theme and do so in stylistically varied form. The following unit (42:18–44:23) proceeds to describe various divine gifts which enable Jacob-Israel to carry out the mandate.

The Introduction of the Servant (41:1–20)

A variety of motifs is employed in order to present Jacob-Israel to the audience. There is first the call to "islands and peoples" to consider the power which stands behind the victorious and world-shaking campaigns of the Persian King Cyrus. It is, so the prophet boldly affirms, no one but the God of Israel (1–5)—certainly not human-made idols (6–7).

The preacher may wish to select the central paragraph as the basis for a sermon. Here Israel-Jacob is addressed by the Lord as "my servant," descended from "Abraham, my beloved one" (8–13). The election motif is dominant and evidently draws its theme and its persuasiveness from the patriarchal traditions in Genesis. Its narratives deal extensively with the Lord's election and protection of Abraham, singling him out from the descendants of Noah and making him and Sarah the parents of Isaac, through whom the Lord's full blessing is to be conveyed to all nations (Gen 12:1–3; 21:8; 24:35). In turn, of Isaac's two sons it was not Esau but Jacob who became the bearer of that blessing. Did he not find himself protected as well as tested on the long journey—in both time and space—which he had to undertake from Canaan to his uncle Laban and back, emerging with a new name and at peace with both brother and uncle (Gen 25:19—35:29)? Does that name not identify him as uniquely claimed by God (Gen 28:20–22; 35:1–15)?

A homily may also deal with the unworthiness of Jacob-Israel as instrument of divine action. The stories in Genesis are both illustration and commentary. They know of Jacob's (and his mother's) conspiracy to lay claim to a blessing not his own unless the father freely bestows it. They also tell of the manner in which he, the man who cheated his firstborn brother, is himself cheated by being given the firstborn sister of Rachel, for whom Jacob had served seven years. They narrate how his shrewdness eventually allows him to leave his uncle's service a very well-to-do man. Esau and Laban, both close relatives as well as adversaries, were not able to thwart the divine will and so demonstrate why Jacob is exhorted "not to fear"—the Lord "has helped" him (10, 13). Is the Israel addressed by the prophet not now engaged in a similar journey to the land of promise? But unlike Father Jacob, who as merely one family made his way to Canaan, the remnant people Jacob-Israel are called "from the ends of the earth" (9; compare 11:11–12; 27:12–13; 60:1–22).

The last two paragraphs are words of encouragement directed either to "little worm Jacob" (14–16) or to "the poor and the deprived" (17–21). The first text speaks twice of "the Holy One of Israel"; it is the Isaianic guide-phrase which uniquely characterizes Isa 1—66 (compare 20 and see the Introduction). Thus titled, the Lord is "your redeemer" (14). Here the prophet-visionary introduces an epithet of the God of Israel which from now on appears often in Isaiah, either as noun or as verb. Its use is foreshadowed, as it were, in a song of celebration with which "the redeemed of the Lord" come to Zion (35:1–10; compare Ps 122). The notion of "redemption" is illustrated by the story of Ruth (see especially 3—4) and by the regulations relating to the buying back of property (see Lev 25:47–55, 25, 28). In Isaiah the motif is used metaphorically to describe the liberation which Israel experiences as a divine action; it is comparable to the legal practice of redeeming persons or property which have become separated from their original (and therefore true) owners.

The blooming of the wilderness is the theme of the last paragraph (17–20). The imagery contrasts the proverbial drought and sterility of the desert with the abundance of water which will be available, and the sparse vegetation with the variety of trees which will grow. But who are the destitute of Israel, now perishing of thirst? Passages such as 35:1–10 and 40:3–5 suggest that they are pilgrims and returnees who, unlike their forebears on their desert journey from Egypt (Exod 15:22–25; Num 20:2–10), have water to spare.

However, since no reference to a journey appears in the text, one wonders whether the paragraph does not describe figuratively—and affirmatively—the formation of diaspora congregations "in the wilderness," that is, in the lands and cities of the dispersion (compare Ezek 20:35 for the metaphorical use of "wilderness" for "place of exile," and Isa 55:1–3 as well as Amos 8:11 for the figurative employment of "thirst" for "longing for divine sustenance"). At any rate, whether abroad or at home, the divine intervention lets gardens of plenty appear out of destruction and chaos—a matter for reflection in light of that motif throughout the Bible (compare 20 and 55:12–13 with Gen 2:8–14; Ezek 47:1–12; Zech 14:8; and Rev 22:1–5).

The Vindication of the Servant (41:21—42:4)

As elsewhere in 40—55, the texts seek to persuade their readers and do so by employing a variety of motifs and styles. Here challenge gives way to pleading, then to demonstration. Thus, the idols are called to court to be examined (41:21–24), are confronted with the evidence of their powerlessness (41:25–28), and are finally referred to the people Jacob-Israel as the Lord's servant who will, through a patient, gentle bearing, seal the Lord's mandate (42:1–4). The following paragraphs proceed to spell out that mandate more fully (42:5–17).

Preachers may explore the repudiated notion that human-made images are of any value. The polemic of the Scriptures against idolatry is well known (compare 40:18–20; 44:9–20); it suggests that idolatry was a temptation to which Israelites and Judaites could and did succumb. The household gods of Laban which Rachel stole are an illustration (Gen 31:30–35), as are "the gods" which Jacob's family members are ordered to give up before they go to Bethel (Gen 35:1–4). Moses' farewell speech stresses that at the holy mountain in the wilderness Israel heard only the Lord's voice. Thus the mediation of the divine presence to the people occurred exclusively through words of assurance and obligation (see Deut 4:11–13, 15–20, 33–36). Just as "signs and portents" vindicated the Lord's words then (Deut 4:34), so also now the prophetic words are proven by a sign: it is the fulfillment of the announcement already made (and written in Isa 13:1—14:23) that Babylon will fall through the victory of "one from the North and the East" (41:25). In other words, the book itself presents the evidence of prediction come true; it does so in a way similar to the "announcement–fulfillment" pattern in "The Former Prophets" (compare 1 Kings 13:1–3 with 2 Kings 23:15–16).

Bruised reed and dimly burning wick, worldwide mission and gentle servant—memorable images describe the mandate of the servant people (42:1–4). The faithful remnant is given the divine spirit and sent across lands and seas to "the people," to the descendants of Father Jacob. Those given that commission are addressed as if they were one person—a familiar feature in Isaiah and elsewhere in scriptural poetry. This is the notion of "corporate personality" (H. Wheeler Robinson), according to which a group is thought of as one person and named so as to suggest its identity. An example is "daughter of Zion," referring to Jerusalem and its inhabitants (16:1; 52:2; Jer 4:31). Hence the fluidity with which biblical texts refer to a community both as made up of individual members and as representing one personal entity; this can also be observed in Isaianic descriptions of "the servant of the Lord."

A homily may deal with the manner in which the servant's mission is executed. The text shows that those commissioned go about their work quietly and persistently, building on their audience's knowledge of sacred tradition and pleading for a hearing. The servant alludes to what the hearers remember of Abraham and Sarah and especially of Jacob, whose "given" name, "Israel," they share (51:1–3; 41:8–13) or of divinely wrought reversals of Israel's, Judah's, and Jerusalem's fate (7:1–9; 36:1–37:38). Through the servant's appeal to memory and goodwill, divinely sanctioned commandment and new instruction (1, 4) establish themselves anew among the dispersed and disheartened; eventually compositions such as the Book of Isaiah or the more comprehensive "Book of Remembrance" will establish themselves among them as spiritual guides and mainstays.

The Commission of the Servant (42:5-17)

Variations in perspective and style also mark the three paragraphs of this passage: here the Lord's word defining the servant's mission (5-9), there the quotation of "the new song" which the divine intervention evokes (10-13), and finally a meditation in which the God of Israel accounts for the action which now gives sight to "the blind" (14-17).

"Covenant mediator" as well as "light to the nations"—these are the tasks which define more precisely the servant's mandate. It is twofold. On the one hand, the remnant is sent to the other members of its people "in order to raise up the tribes of Jacob" (49:6), that is, to reclaim them for the religion of their forebears and for worship on Mount Zion—just as King Josiah had done two or three generations earlier (2 Kings 23:19-23; compare also 2 Chron 30:1—31:1). In this manner the remnant becomes the agent through which the divine covenant with Israel as "a kingdom of priests and a holy nation" (Exod 19:5-6; compare 1 Peter 2:1-5 and Rev 5:9-10) is reenacted.

On the other hand, the servant's second mandate, to be "a light to the nations," affirms the first. It reaches beyond the circle of Jacob's kin and seeks the descendants of Isaac and Rebekah, of Abraham, Hagar, Sarah, and Keturah, even of Noah and his three sons. They all are addressed, it seems, because their memories and rites relate them also to Jacob-Israel's people, their younger brothers and sisters as it were (see Gen 6—35). In their positive response to the missionaries from Jacob-Israel "their eyes are opened" (7); they turn from their idolatrous religious practices to that one divine Lord whose word has announced both "the former things" (Jerusalem's earlier rescues) and now also "the new ones" (the present reversal of Zion's fate; see 40:1-2, 9-11; 52:7-9).

A sermon may also deal with the theme of restored Israel's "new song" (10-13). This is the people's response, acknowledging the new which their divine master has done (compare 43:16-20) and doing so appropriately with a song not heard before (compare 12:1-6 and 35:16-20). It contrasts with Israel's "old" song, which celebrates the deliverance from Egyptian bondage (Exod 15:1–18). The new song exceeds the old, even as the present and future ingathering of the dispersed from all the directions of the compass goes beyond the old ingathering from the land of the pharaohs. Yet both songs celebrate the Lord as "a man of war" (13; compare Exod 15:3). Thus, they contrast starkly with the servant's gentleness and his acceptance of suffering and death (42:2–4; 52:13—53:12). Readers note that both motifs continue to appear in scriptural traditions, one in expressions of the supremacy of Israel's God, the other in calls to peacemaking (compare Rev 11:17–18 with Matt 5:9 and Pirqe Aboth 1:12).

Divine endurance of human blindness finally at an end and people without sight led into light—the images of the last paragraph (14–17) also suggest a sermon topic. Here the word "blind" functions as guideword, readying the audience for the presentation of various gifts through which the God of Israel will enlighten and equip the servant people (42:18—44:23). The new word which Jacob-Israel is given to announce and to act out is available only to those who let their minds be illuminated so as to recognize the deeper, spiritual dimension of what they perceive. Does Israel not find itself time and again offered the divine gift of new ears and eyes, of a heart circumcised (compare Deut 29:1–3 and Jer 4:3–4 with Isa 6:8, 10, and see Mark 4:9, 10–12)?

The Gift of Sight to the Servant (42:18—44:23)

How will the servant's blindness be overcome? The central section of the passage (43:1—44:20) outlines no fewer than five gifts, each giving a greater insight than the preceding one (43:1–7, 14–15, 16–21; 44:1–5, 6–20). Introduced by an appeal to the nations who still find themselves in darkness and distance from the God of Israel (42:18–25), punctuated by appeal and chastisement (44:8–13, 22–28), and (like the preceding unit) concluded with a summary review and a brief song of celebration (44:21–22, 23), the passage describes what it takes to become the carrier of the mandate of the servant: insight into the secret of the divine counsel. "Do you not perceive it . . . ?" (43:19).

The Repentance of the Servant (42:18–25)

"It is nobody but the Lord against whom we have sinned ..." (24b). The servant people have been chosen not because of any merit of their own—on the contrary! The divine appeal to the deaf and blind remnant paints their condition with candor. They see and hear many things but do not perceive their true significance. They are plundered and displaced but do not recognize the real cause. However, confronted by the direct question, "Who has handed Israel to its raiders?", they respond with a confession of their apostasy. It is only then— privileged by hindsight, as it were—that a deeper understanding is attained.

The preacher may wish to explore the realistic portrayal of the change in perception which an informed retrospective brings. According to Zech 1:1–16 "the earlier prophets" tried unsuccessfully to call Israel away from its apostasies. The prophetic voice of our text affirms that it is now the task of a new generation to learn "not to be like their fathers" (Zech 1:4; compare Amos 4:6–12). What distinguishes the Lord's servant, however, is the notion that the insight into Israel's failure is not withheld but is granted here and now. Does not the mandate given to the prophet long ago speak of the termination of the people's deaf and blind state once banishment and desolation have gone once, even twice, over land and people (6:11–13)? By the same token, the insight which liberates human beings for spiritual service is here seen no more as a gift of the future; it is available to the prophet's audience today.

Five Gifts of Insight (43:1—44:20)

The sustained text-cluster presents an almost bewildering picture. How to order the variety of its motifs and images, of its styles and moods? The Lord's call to Israel, appearing at the end of the unit and exhorting it to "remember these (things)" (44:21), sums up and concludes the preceding paragraphs. The latter outline several aspects of the insight needed for the mission, and do so after the servant people has become ready to listen (42:18–25). There is (1) the recognition of the Lord's protection of the people in the vicissitudes of their past (43:1–7; compare 8–13), then (2) the latest proof of that divine care manifest in the Lord's humiliation of Babylon (43:14–15), followed by (3) the description of "the new (things)" which the Lord is doing now (43:16–21; compare 22–28), and by (4) the announcement of the outpouring of divine spirit and blessing (44:1–5), concluded by (5) the portrayal of the stark contrast between human-made idols and the Lord who is "first and last" (44:6–8, 9–20).

(1) A sermon may explore the manner in which the first paragraph summarily and pointedly draws on the hearer's memory of the traditions about Israel's history, transmitted by earlier generations. There is the doubled reference to the Lord as Jacob-Israel's "creator" (1a, 7; the parallel formulations employ both verbs used in Gen 1:2—2:4a / 2:4b–25 in order to refer to the divine activity of creation, that is, "to create," as well as "to form, give shape to"). There is the allusion to the divine naming of Jacob (1b; compare Gen 32:22–32; also 25:26). Then there is the mention of waters and rivers safely traversed (2a; compare Exod 15:19–20; Josh 4:21–24) and of threatening fire from which Israel was protected (2b; compare Exod 19:18–23; also Lev 10:1–2). Also, there is the emphasis on the Lord's holiness (3a; compare Lev 19:2; Num 20:13), as well as on the divine "exchange" of Egypt for Israel (3b; compare Exod 15:19). Finally, the affirmation of the Lord's love as the mainspring of the election of Israel is familiar from Moses' farewell speech (4a; compare Deut 4:37, 7:13), as is the divine exhortation "not to fear" (1b, 5a; compare Deut 1:21; 3:22). The recognition of the correspondence between the prophet's review of past manifestations of the divine presence with Jacob-Israel and the relevant passages in "The Law" (Genesis–Deuteronomy) is a fitting first gift of insight. It provides the foundation for insights which follow.

A homily may deal with the world-embracing perspective of the text. Both men and women (6b) will gather for pilgrimage to or settlement in the land of promise; they will come from East and West, North and South. Evidently Judaites and Israelites, not to mention their relatives descended from Isaac and Abraham, have moved, voluntarily or involuntarily, to other locations. Thus Solomon's Temple dedication prayer refers to non-Israelites coming to worship from lands far away (1 Kings 8:41–43); moreover, "a Book of Remembrance" tells of many deportations, flights, or escapes of individuals or groups: Mesopotamia (Gen 27:42–45), Assyria (2 Kings 15:29; 17:6), Babylonia (2 Kings 24:14–16; 25:21), and Egypt (1 Kings 11:40; 2 Kings 23:34). While migrations to lands across the Mediterranean Sea are not well attested (but compare Isa 66:19), several references to seafaring (1 Kings 10:22; Jon; Ps 107:23–30) suggest that Israelites and Judaites came to settle in the sixth and fifth centuries B.C.E. on "the islands," that is, Mediterranean shore cities (compare Isa 41:1; 42:4).

On the other hand, the Lord's presence with Israel from creation on, as it were, can and must be attested by the people (8–13). They are, so the God of Israel affirms, "my witnesses" (10, 12; compare 44:8). There is no other God whom they may credit with their protection—do not their stories and songs portray the God of Israel from of old as their Lord and King (Exod 15:18–Deut 6:4)?

(2) The second gift of insight is simply and briefly identified. It is the Lord's intervention on Israel's behalf in the immediate past, that is, Babylon's overthrow (14–15) carried out through the Persian King Cyrus, the Lord's "anointed one" (45:1). Foretold as such (13:1–14:23) and anticipated in the prophet's announcement of a future exile of Judah to that city (39:1–8), it provides the opportunity to the exiled people to return to their land for rebuilding on the ancient foundations. Small wonder that later in the book the urgent call is heard, "Depart! Depart! Go out from there"(52:11–12). The Lord thus claims once again the royal role of which the Song of the Sea (Exod 15:1–18) already knows.

(3) The third gift of insight is related to the present (16–21). After aspects of the divine presence since creation have been outlined (1–7) and the recent humiliation of Babylon mentioned (14–15), the passage calls for the servant's insight into the new thing which the Lord is now doing. With a power greater than it took to overcome Egypt's might (16–17; compare 18), the Lord sets about to transform that wilderness which Israel had dreaded on leaving Egypt (Deut 1:19), and which had exacted a terrible toll from them (Deut 1:34–38), into a place of delight. Not only will it have road and spring,

but even its wild animals will honor the Lord. These marvels will be accomplished, so the Lord affirms, "in order to give drink to my chosen people" (19–20).

The preacher cannot help but note the way in which this second exodus is portrayed with the colors of the first. But it transcends that journey in that it becomes enjoyable and is no more a mortal test of forty years. Moreover, the description of the desert may also suggest that it is metaphoric—references to it as well as to "thirst" and its quenching are used to allude to a divinely blessed life in the diaspora among its congregations (see Ezek 20:35; Amos 8:11 and comments on 41:1–20).

Hardly a sharper contrast can be imagined than the one between this announcement of the new order (16–21) and the following condemnation of Israel's lack of loyalty in the past (22–28). The guideword "weary" appears three times (22, 23b, 24b); the verb form "to make somebody serve" is used twice (23b, 24b), the second reversing the subject and object of the first. The Lord "has not made Israel serve with (ritual) gifts," but Israel "has made the Lord serve for its sins."

However, the nature of the people's failure is not clearly described in 22–28. It seems that the condemnation is directed against "selective obedience" (see 1:10–17), that is, cultic observances which are not born of a spirit of integrity. It is thus not a condemnation of the cult as such (compare Amos 5:21–25 and Hos 6:6). This interpretation agrees with the negative view of "your first father," evidently Jacob (compare Hos 12:2–3), and of "your spokesmen," presumably kings, priests, and prophets who act contrary to the divine will (compare 1 Kings 11:1–10; Isa 28:7–8). One notes that the memory of father Jacob presents both positive and negative features—in keeping with his portrayal in Gen 25–50.

(4) The fourth gift to the servant is that of the Lord's spirit and blessing (44:1–5; especially 3b). Again the image of water poured on dry land (3a; compare 43:20) introduces the promise. As a result, Jacob-Israel's descendants will sprout like grass and willow growing next to channels of water (4; compare Ps 1:3a), profess their allegiance to the Lord, and identify themselves openly as members of Jacob-Israel (5; compare 19:18).

The preacher notes that the passage speaks of nothing less than a new creation. As in one of the creation stories (Gen 1:2), so also here the divine spirit is pictured at work. It is the agent of the Lord's creative as well as re-creative activity (compare 32:15; 42:1; 61:1–3; Jer 31:31–34; Ezek 37:1–14; Joel 3:1–2; and Acts 2:1–4). Similarly, the gift of blessing, paralleled with that of the spirit, describes the state of well-being, harmony, and peace which marks creation in its wholeness (Gen 1:22, 28; 2:3; 9:1) and which God's people both enjoy and give to others (Gen 12:1–3; Num 6:24–26).

(5) The final insight given to the servant is the certainty that the Lord is the only God (6–8), in comparison to whom human-made images of the divine offer no help and pale into oblivion (9–20). Here the preacher notes the emphasis in the doubled quotation of the Lord's word that "there is no God except for me" (6b, 8b). This is what Israel as "witnesses of the Lord" (8b; compare 43:10, 12) is called to attest; it fittingly concludes the series of insights which empower the servant. Accordingly, the Lord is "first and last" (6b)—a claim readily understandable in light of the preceding arguments.

A sermon may focus on the zeal with which the argument for "monotheism" is made. The following exposé of the folly of the manufacture and use of images provides a foil for the argument. It suggests that its addressees are Israelites and Judaites who have and use images, made as described in 9–20. Narratives such as Gen 31:30–35; 35:1–4 and Judg 8:24–27 imply that the possession of images by Israelites is a matter of the past, a practice relinquished long ago and not a temptation any more. However, the repeated warnings against their production and use in "The Law" (for example, Exod 20:4–6 [=Deut 5:8–10]; 20:19–20; 34:17; Deut 4:15–24; compare Jer 10:1–16) and the outright prediction of Moses in his farewell speech to the effect that Israel, when scattered due to its idolatry, will have no choice but "to serve gods of wood and stone" (Deut 4:28) suggest that the cultic use of images was widespread, or at least a constant temptation. Moreover, archaeological finds of (metal) images of gods or their animals and of (clay) fertility figurines indicate that these religious objects were in use.

Whatever the exact historical conditions may have been, 6–

8 plead the superior and all-encompassing nature of Israel's God, denying divine rank to any competitor. Arguments such as these in Ps 82 and Deut 4 (compare 1 Kings 22 and Job 1—2) show, on the other hand, that debates about quantifiable aspects of the divine left their traces. It is noteworthy that already the creation stories with which the Scriptures begin, and which set the stage for what follows, imply a certain plurality within the divine unity. Thus, according to Gen 1:26 the creator addresses fellow divine beings when commanding the human being to come into existence, and Gen 2:4b–24 implies a certain divine attribute to Adam and Eve after they have tasted the fruit of the tree of knowledge. There is no doubt, however, that the affirmation of God's unity dominates early Jewish and Christian reflection on the divine (compare Deut 6:4; Mark 12:29; but also John 10:31–38 and its use of Ps 82:6).

The Celebration of the New Redemption (44:21–23)

Text clusters in Isaiah frequently conclude on a high note. So also here, Jacob-Israel is called to "remember these (insights)" and not to forget its divine master. After all, the God of Israel has "wiped away like a cloud your acts of disloyalty" and thus "redeemed you." Repetitions make for emphasis: "Jacob/Israel" (21, 23), "servant" (21a, b), and "redeeming" (22b, 23c). They bring to a climax the paragraphs which precede and set the stage for what follows: the details of the restoration to come (44:24–46:13) and of Babylon's humiliation (47:1–15).

A homily may note the exuberance of the response to the Lord's saving intervention—a familiar pattern in the Scriptures (compare Exod 15:1–18; Judg 5:1–31; 1 Sam 2:1–10; 2 Sam 22:1–51; Isa 12:1–6; 35:1–10; 55:1–13) not to mention the doxologies in the liturgies of synagogues and churches. Striking is the call to the sky and to the earth's depths, to the mountains and the trees, to sing the praise of the Lord—reminder that all creation is included in the redemptive activity of the divine (compare 11:1–9; 55:12; Ezek 47:1–12; Rom 8:19–23; and Rev 22:1–5).

The Re-creation of Jacob-Israel (44:24—46:13)

"Cyrus, my shepherd and my anointed one" (44:28; 45:1) is the surprising opener of the passage, and the affirmation of the Lord's preservation of Israel "until grey hair" (46:4), its reassuring conclusion. Here the double miracle of the people's rebirth and of its ingathering from the four corners of the earth is announced. The text first deals with the Persian order to rebuild Jerusalem and its temple, given by the Persian king, and the prophet's defense of that divine action against detractors (44:24—45:13). Then it moves to the world-spanning invitation addressed to Israel's descendants, calling for their return to Jerusalem as pilgrim worshipers (45:14–25). It concludes with the assertion of the Lord's preservation of the remnant people "from womb to old age" (46:1–13). In this text a variety of moods and styles makes for a lively combination of motifs and images.

The Refounding of Jerusalem (44:24—45:13)

Twice the Lord's word to Israel is conveyed through the prophet. The first announces Cyrus' rebuilding order (24–28), and the second assures the people that the divine action, carried out through the Persian ruler, is in fact accomplished not for Cyrus' but for Israel's sake (1–8). Finally, the prophet counters those who oppose that conviction (9–13).

A homily may explore the claim that the God of Israel does not intervene directly but acts through the agency of great powers on the world's stage. Do the latter not seem to be the ones who take the initiative and shape events as it suits them? Does the evidence not support that view? But the insight given prophets allows them to see further and to perceive in the ups and downs of Israel, Judah, and the nations a divine plan at work. The parable of the farmer (28:23–29) illustrates the long-range goal orientation of the Lord's counsel. Do not prophetic speeches repeatedly portray Assyrian and Babylonian potentates as "rods of divine anger" and "servants of the Lord" (10:5–6; Jer 25:9–10)? Now the Persian king is even honored with titles usually reserved for faithful kings of Judah! Thus, David was commissioned to "shepherd the people of God" and was described as "the anointed one" (2 Sam 5:2; 3:39).

If the audience is tempted to doubt the Lord's appointment of Cyrus as "my shepherd," let it note the manner in which the Lord prefaces that decree: there are references to the Lord's exclusive action in creation (24b; compare Gen 2:4b–25), to the divine confounding of wise men (25; compare Gen 41:8; Exod 7:11), to the Lord's drying out rivers (27; compare Exod 15:19; Josh 5:1) and, to clinch the argument, to the fulfillment of promises made to the Lord's servant (26a; compare 13:1—14:23; and generally Zech 1:1–6).

Not only does the description of the Lord's guidance of Cyrus mention "the treasures of darkness" given over to the victor (45:1–3a); it also asserts that the king himself is unaware of what Israel is told: not he, but Israel's God is the one at work (45:3b–5). Since the Lord is the only supreme power, darkness and evil also must be understood as caused by the God of Israel (45:6–8; contrast Gen 1:2—2:4a)!

Finally, the preacher notes that the prophet's bold assertion does not go unchallenged. Those who oppose it are confronted with two rhetorical questions (9–10), then addressed with the divine assurance that it is indeed the God of Israel who through Cyrus releases the exiled and reverses the fate of their holy city, doing so unconditionally (11–13).

The Worldwide Invitation (45:14–25)

"Turn to me and let yourselves be helped, all ends of the earth!" (22a). This is the theme which dominates the unit. It begins with the Lord's announcement that Egypt's wealth and Cush's trade goods will be brought to Jerusalem by pilgrims who confess that only here do they encounter God's presence (14–17). Then a further divine announcement (18–19) counters claims made by adversaries to the effect that the land, recently laid waste, is and remains precisely that: a place condemned to obscurity and darkness—like the primal chaos of which Gen 1:2 speaks with (a part of) the same word. But that very reference to chaos points to the divine activity which overcomes it: the command which establishes order and so creates the terrestrial sphere, destined for human habitation. Thus the call to all of Jacob's descendants can be sounded; they are urged to become exclusive worshipers of the Lord (20-25).

A sermon may explore the claim that the Lord's responsibility for all that happens can be perceived only by Israel when illumined by the prophet's word. Since the human agents are admittedly unaware of this, the prophet interjects the affirmation "you are a God who hides himself, O God of Israel, its helper" (15). In other words, the insight into the Lord's guidance of the affairs of creation lies hidden, as it were, within the small and scattered remnant people. This is Israel's way of coping with reality and claiming for itself a future.

Thus the missionary call of 20-25, addressed to "the escaped from the nations," urges them to forsake other forms of devotion to the divine and become adherents of the Lord (compare a similar thrust in the Apostle Paul's use of the motif in Phil 2:5-11). Since "Israel's seed" is invited, heterodox practices followed by (some of?) them seem to be the target. For further observations, see the comments above on 44:6-20; also note that Exod 6:2 is aware of earlier, different revelations to Israel's ancestors and equates them with the revelation of the Lord to Moses. On the other hand, narratives such as Gen 35:1-4 and Judg 8:24-27 (compare Gen 31:30-35) suggest that images of the divine were part of religious practice of some of Jacob's kin.

The Preservation of Israel (46:1-13)

Here Babylon's idols "carried by tired beasts of burden," there renewed Israel "carried" by the Lord safely "into old age"—the contrast sets the tone for the passage. Bel and Nebo, well-known gods of the Babylonian pantheon, have to stoop low (1-2), while the Lord's people raises itself high, assured of God's lasting support (3-4). In a further play on two words for "carrying," the powerlessness of images is caricatured; they need to be borne on the shoulder, and even when they are set down, they must be secured lest they topple (5-7). The concluding paragraph (8-13) reviews several of the arguments presented earlier in 40:1—45:7, appealing to the "self-confident" in Israel to "remember" the manifest fulfillment of the Lord's words spoken in the past.

A sermon may explore the theme of comfort which the notion of the Lord's "carrying" the servant people "from mother's womb to grey hair" offers to all its members (3–4). Israel and Judah have experienced both prosperity and deprivation, blessing and despair. Assured of new beginnings when all seemed lost and they displaced, they have come to know the divine desire for their peace and well-being. Does the familiar picture of each person being at ease under vine and figtree (1 Kings 5:5; Zech 3:10) not point to that same rest of the creature within creation?

The Humiliation of the Mistress of Kingdoms (47:1–15)

"Come down and sit in the dust, maiden daughter of Babylon!" The prophet addresses the fallen world power who had humbled Judah without showing mercy. Vignette follows vignette: Babylon's removal from the exalted seat of power (1–4), review of her arrogant words (5–7) and boundless self-assurance (8–10a), her futile reliance on magicians (10n–12) and horoscope interpreters (13–15). Through these words speaks the soul of a people released from cruelty and oppression, reassuring itself that what has been foretold of old has now been fulfilled (compare 13:1—14:23). Thus the dirgelike composition comes to stand as the conclusion of the larger text unit which introduces the Lord's third and final rescue of the holy city (38 / 40—47).

The lively tone of the composition invites the preacher's attention. It is a sequence of reproachfully but also sympathetically spoken words, given rhythm through changes in style and addressee. There are quotations of smug expressions of Babylon's deluded sense of security; there are outright affirmations that "it's all over," as well as ironic request and grateful acknowledgment. Then there is the motif that Babylon has exceeded the limits set for her: even though the Lord gave Judah into her power, she made the "yoke heavy also on the old" (6). Was not Assyria also castigated for the same failure to recognize its bounds (10:5–19)?

A sermon may reflect on the manner in which the prophetic book portrays the pattern of divine promise and fulfillment, evident in each of its three parts. There is the first escape of

Jerusalem from a dire threat, announced and fulfilled (7:1-9). Then, a generation later, the second escape, this time from the Assyrians (36:1—37:38). Now also the third—and greatest—rescue is assured: Babylon has fallen!

The Call of Abraham's Kin (48:1—55:13)

"It is too little that you should raise up the tribes of Jacob ... therefore I appoint you light of the nations. . . ." (49:6). At first the mission of the remnant people is limited to its own, as yet unillumined, members (40:1—47:15), but now it is extended to include "nations," that is, those related to Jacob's kin because they are descendants of Abraham (compare 51:1-2 with Gen 12:1-3). In other words, the enlarged mandate of the Lord's servant will bring together what in the course of scriptural narration (Gen 11—35) became separated: the descendants of Ishmael, of Isaac, and of Keturah, as well as Esau's kin. Thus, this second segment of Isaiah's third part is one of the units within Scripture which set the stage for the eventual reconciliation of "fathers and sons, sons and fathers" (Mal 4:6), overcoming the legacy of alienation of which the Bible's opening narratives already speak (compare further 55:1-13; 60:1-22; 66:22-23; Ezek 47:1-12; 1 Cor 15:51-57; Col 1:15-20; and Rev 21:1-22:5).

The first unit (48:1-22) focuses on the theme of Jacob's redemption; it looks back on what precedes and introduces the greater redemption to come. The second passage (49:1—50:11) spells out the servant people's expanded mandate and shows what that requires of them. The third text (51:1—52:6) evokes the memory of Abraham and Sarah and proceeds to compare refounded Zion to the Garden of Eden. Then both the agony and the reward of Israel's mission, faithfully carried out, are probed (52:7—53:12). Finally, the Lord's "eternal covenant of peace" and its invitation to those who "thirst" (54:1—55:13) are celebrated.

The Redemption of Jacob-Israel (48:1-22)

From castigation to consolation—more than twice the passage moves through the compositional rhythm which characterizes the book (compare 1-8, 17-19, and 22 with 9-16 and

20–21). Moreover, the text is a summary review of important themes in 40–47, placed here as the basis for the expanded mission of Jacob-Israel (49:1—50:11). Thus, there appears the emphasis on the Lord's presence throughout time and space, whether as the one divine power who alone and truthfully announced of old through prophet's mouth what is to come (3, 6; compare 41:1–5; 43:16–21; 44:6–8; 46:8–13), or as the one who is "first and last," that is, supreme in divine status (12; compare 40:12–26; 44:6–8).

On the other hand, there is the urgent call to "go forth" from Babylon, now that Cyrus no longer holds the exiles captive and thus opens the way for the new which the Lord is doing (20–21; compare 45:13; 52:11–12). The people are assured that be they returnees or pilgrims, their journey is not only a greater exodus than the one of which inherited stories tell, but also one marked by ease and joy (21; compare 40:3–5; 43:20; also 35:1–10; 55:1–13; and 60:1–22).

The preacher notes that the Lord quotes Israel's words which indicate its eagerness to attribute the release from captivity to their "idol, be it shaped or molten image" (5b). Does the prophet indeed portray the servant people as outrightly idolatrous? And if so, how may that be explained in light of the avowedly "aniconic" conceptualization of the divine in the Hebrew Scriptures? Already the texts of 44:6–20 and 45:20–25 deal with this issue; see the comments offered there.

A sermon may deal with the notion of the gift of the divine spirit, suggested by the interjection in 16c: "My Lord, the Lord (literally: Yahweh, the probably pronunciation of the proper name of Israel's God) has sent me, and (has endowed me with) his spirit." Several passages in Isaiah throw light on this text, notably 11:2 (1–9), 31:3 (1–3), 44:3 (1–5), 59:21, and 61:1–3. They indicate that the endowment with the celestial spirit empowers those given mandates to carry them out, be they kings, prophets, or a people. At times this draws ridicule (compare Hos 9:7), and it can set spirit people apart from their contemporaries (compare 8:16–18; 59:21; Jer 14:15–18). By the same token, the reception of the spirit by all of God's people is desired already by Moses (Num 11:29 (4–34); compare Joel 3:1–2 and Acts 2:1–42).

The Servant's Greater Mandate (49:1—50:11)

The "new thing" that the Lord is doing (compare 43:19) includes a task which so far has only been mentioned but not laid out: the extension of the mission to those beyond the circle of Jacob-Israel (compare 42:6 [1–9] with 49:6 [1–7]). There is first the full announcement of that change (49:1–13), then the description of Zion's surprise over the arrival of the unexpected worshipers from afar (49:14—50:3), concluded by an exploration of the greater cost of discipleship which this change brings for the servant people (50:4–11).

The Inclusion of Separated Kin (49:1–13)

In broad strokes 1–6 reviews the servant people's appeal to islands and peoples, demanding that they take note of its ancient, God-given role among them. Though "hidden like an arrow in the Lord's quiver" and tempted to relinquish the frustrating task, the servant proceeds to announce the Lord's decree of the extension of the original mandate: he is to be "a light of nations," so that "my salvation may reach to the end of the earth." The reversal of Israel's humiliated condition is as surprising as that of its inherited land (7, 8–13).

The preacher notes motifs which suggest sermon topics. The "universalism" of the servant's newly defined mission stands out. Rather than interpreting the term in a broad, undifferentiated manner, readers acquainted with the Scriptures recognize the manner in which the text takes up and inverts the theme of the gradual separation of Abraham's, Sarah's, and Keturah's descendants from each other, one of whom is Jacob, their tribal ancestor. Do not stories tell of Ishmael's departure from his father's presence (Gen 16:1–15; 21:9–21), even though he is included in the covenant of circumcision (Gen 17:23–27)? Were not Abraham's sons by Keturah "sent eastward, away from his (Abraham's) son Isaac" (Gen 25:1–6)? Do not the Jacob / Esau narratives tell in painful detail of the alienation between the twin brothers (Gen 25:19—36:43)?

Thus, a sermon may show how this text (as several comparable ones; see introduction to 48:1—55:13) seeks to heal what has been broken and to bring together again those who are descended of Abraham, "the Lord's beloved one" (51:2). Moreover, do not stories found in "The Prophets" also illustrate the separations which rivalry, enmity, or lack of mutual loyalty effect between siblings (compare, for example, Judg 12:1–6; 19:1—21:25; 2 Sam 8:9–14; 1 Kings 15:16–22; Obad)? Thus, the great restoration which is now beginning includes not only the descendants of Israel's twelve sons but also of their fellow tribes; wherever they may reside, they are invited to claim with the servant people their place in the light of the Lord (compare 60:1–22).

A preacher may also deal with the vexing question of the identity of the servant. It has long been a matter of reflection in both synagogues and churches. Does not a well-to-do Ethiopian pilgrim in the first century of our era, on his return journey from Jerusalem reading in the prophetic book a similar passage about the servant's suffering (52:13–54:12), already puzzle over the question (Acts 8:34 [26–39])? Small wonder that many Christian interpreters have since held that the figure is an individual (and points to Jesus)—after all, several passages speak of that person in the singular (see 42:1–4; 50:4–9 and the text that pilgrim was reading). Moreover, 49:6 assigns to the servant a task to be done in (or to) Israel, not to mention the modern thesis that four texts in 40–55 should be separated from their contexts and as "Servant Songs" refer to an individual (42:1–4; 49:1–6; 50:4–9; 52:13—53:12).

On the other hand, most Jewish but also some Christian interpreters are persuaded that the servant is none other than the remnant of Israel, who has remained loyal to the God of Israel and been reassured in its faithfulness through prophetic activity such as that of Isaiah and Jeremiah. Thus they advocate a "collective" understanding. This position, adopted here, is explained by the notion of "corporate personality" (H. Wheeler Robinson). According to it a community or a city may be seen both as "many" and as "one," both as a group with many members and as an individual figure; note the phrase "daughter of Zion," used to refer to the inhabitants of the city as well as to the city, and see the comments made in relation to 41:21—42:4.

The Surprise of a Deserted Mother (49:14—50:3)
In three paragraphs one theme is unfolded: the amazing reversal of Zion's fate. Portrayed as a "mother," who bore and raised children but then found herself bereft of them and barren (50:1, 49:20), she cannot hold back her surprise when not only are her offspring brought back in honor, but persons she never knew crowd into her tent (49:17, 18, 21–23).

The preacher notes the variety of images which describe the complete change: the lively interaction between quotations of Jerusalem's words of both initial despair and eventual elation (49:14, 21), between the Lord's reassurances and reproachful questioning (49:18; 50:1–12), and between the prophet's reflections and the returnees' demand for more living space (49:15, 20). The conceptual and stylistic freedom of the prophet-visionary is warrant and encouragement for preachers similarly to be inventive and artful in their words—is this not a privilege of those entrusted with the message of reconciliation?

A sermon may explore, on the other hand, the unusual title for the God of Israel with which the second paragraph (49:22–26) concludes: "The Mighty One of Jacob." The phrase is one of the rarer guidewords within the Book of Isaiah, appearing in both prologue and epilogue (1:24; 60:16) as well as here in the third part (49:26). The phrase is seldom used in the Hebrew Bible; except for two occurrences in Ps 132, it is only found in Isaiah and in "The Blessing of Jacob" (Gen 49:24). Readers cannot help but note that the God of Jacob and of his twelve sons is here in a special way related to just one of the sons, to Joseph, the one severely tested in the "exile" to which his brothers abandon him (Gen 37—48). That very Joseph not only eventually forgives his siblings, but also, reflecting on the amazing reversal which their God has wrought, addresses them with the words, "Although you intended me harm, God intended it for good, so as to bring about . . . the survival of many. Hence do not be afraid. I will sustain you and your children" (Gen 50:20–21). These words by a man specially protected by "The Mighty One of Jacob" aptly characterize the Isaianic passage as well.

Reminders of the servant people's lack of response to the divine demands in the past are found in the text as well—in keeping with the compositional pattern outlined in the Introduction. Thus there appears not only the quotation of Israel's despairing words over the lack of success in its mission (49:4a), but also the reference to the dismissal of Jerusalem from the divine presence, due to her failure to live according to the mandate to be a city of justice (50:1; compare 3:8–12, 16–26; 22:1–14). The point is this: it was not the Lord who "divorced" Zion; rather, she divorced herself through her infidelity. The next lines show that her divine master came and sought her but did so in vain (50:2). However, the text concludes with the reassuring, rhetorical question, "Is my hand too short to save?"

The Cost of Discipleship (50:4–11)

The intensity of the servant's words is evident already in the doubling of several words and phrases. No fewer than five appear twice in the text: "disciples," "ear opening/stirring," "in the morning" (or "morning by morning"), "shaming," and "my Lord, the Lord helps me." They indicate that the mandate generates tension and opposition. The servant people (50:10; or is it the prophet who is speaking, merging as it were into the people?) presents itself as instructed daily by its divine master "to encourage the weary" with comforting speech. That activity is resented by adversaries who physically abuse the servant. The servant, however, does not retaliate, secure in the assurance that the Lord's judgment will be the final word on his behalf, while the opponents will vanish. Hence the appeal to those who "fear the Lord," exhorting them not to rely on their own perishable light but to "trust in the Lord's name."

The preacher notes the violent hostility to the Lord's servant as portrayed in the text. Taken aback by such high cost of discipleship, readers wonder what causes the enmity. The book, however, speaks elsewhere of the failure of those addressed to listen to the Lord's claims conveyed by servant and prophet, or of their outright opposition (see 7:10–17; 8:16–18; 45:9–13; 48:1–8; comp. 53:3). Furthermore, words and stories about other servants of the Lord, especially prophets, know of similar adversity, even of martyrdom (1 Kings 19:1–2; 22:8; 2 Kings 6:31; Jer 11:21–22; Amos 7:10–17; especially Jer 26:20–23). Thus Ezekiel describes the prophet of the Lord as the one who is prepared to step into the breaches (in city walls) in order to protect the people (13:5), and the notion of the violent fate of the Lord's servants, the prophets, later becomes a common—and telling—narrative motif (for example, Luke 11:47–51; 13:34).

A sermon will have to deal with the sobering insight that the Scriptures tell of fierce hostility between persons and groups of different religious persuasions, and that many a biblical text is born of religious zeal and polemic. It is doubly puzzling when—as is the case here—the latter are generated by a servant's obedient listening to the divine voice and the words of comfort which flow from it. Is the servant's condemnation of images of the divine, evidently a variant form of cultic practice, the cause? Are the strong affirmations of "my Lord, the Lord" as "first and last" the bone of contention? Does the speaker's intimate, constant, and, it seems, exclusive relationship with the Lord create the hostility? The answer will soon be given: words of derision and acts of maltreatment, which the servant endures, will be recognized by the adversaries and by others as "the chastisement that made us whole" (53:5b)!

Recovery of Creation's Horizons (51:1—52:6)

The poetic exuberance of the passage reaches for mythic imagery coupled with urgent appeals. Few texts in Isa 1—66 equal these lines in the ardor of their arguments and the force of their style. Thus, repeated doublings of words and phrases leave the audience almost breathless. The doubled command "Rise! Rise! Put on strength!" (51:9 and 52:1) frames the call to the city, "Rouse yourself! Rouse yourself! Stand up, Jerusalem!" (51:17). The word pictures are similarly daring. There is the reference to the drying up of "the great deep" and of the defeat of primeval sea monsters, earlier the motif of "the Garden of the Lord" and later in the passage that of "planting heaven and founding earth." Evidently, mythic language seeks to capture Zion's new creation within comprehensive perspectives.

Three aspects of the new creation centered in Zion are described. Its celebration as a return to Eden's realm (51:1–8) is followed by the call on the Lord's power to create anew, through prophet's word, heaven, earth, and Zion (51:9–16). It is that city which is roused and challenged to claim its role as holy center of a world in the making (51:17—52:6). The following passage (52:7—53:12) will again focus on the servant's mission and portray both its promise and its agony.

Return to Eden (51:1–8)

Those who seek the Lord are challenged to "look to the rock from which you were cut, to the quarry from which you were hewn." The identification of Abraham and Sarah in this manner is telling: they are pictured as the archparents of those for whom the book is composed, and it seems that this is equally true of "The Law and the Prophets," in other words, that comprehensive work of which Isa 1—66 is a part (see Introduction). Thus the Abraham/Sarah narration (Gen 12–25) is the scriptural foil against which the passage is to be read. In turn, that narration combines with Gen 1—11 by reversing narratively the brokenness of which that first section tells. Thus the preacher notes in the Isaianic text the very theme of restoration which the Abraham/Sarah narration itself sets against that of the alienation portrayed in Gen 1—11 (see the comments on 49:1–13).

A sermon may also explore the manner in which the servant's worldwide mission is connected to the promulgation and observance of the Lord's law. The people is reminded that from its divine master's mouth proceeds "The Law," offered alike to Israel and to its fellow tribes descended from Abraham. In this fashion it becomes "a light of nations" (4). Here the remnant people's mandate to be "a light to the peoples" is juxtaposed with the equally comprehensive destiny of "The Law."

Readers cannot but note the double emphasis on the external and the internal appropriation of that law: on the one hand, it is carried to the earth's ends, presumably written on scrolls and protected by covers (compare 42:1–4; 49:6). On the other hand, it is also carried "in their hearts," and that by a people in search of justice and righteousness (7; compare

1). Does not Deuteronomy, Moses' farewell speech, time and again seek to instill in its audience the desire to meditate and reflect on "The Law" (Deut 6:4–9; 11:18–22; compare 4:5–8; 17:18–20; 32:45–47)? The dying lawgiver concludes with the affirmation that it is "not too baffling for you nor beyond your reach.... It is very close to you, in your mouth and in your heart" (Deut 30:11–14). Moreover, is not King Josiah's ready acceptance of and missionary activity based on that law, found unexpectedly when the Temple was repaired, an illustration of what the servant people is called to do—not to mention the monarch's command to all Israel that they journey to Jerusalem and celebrate the Passover there (2 Kings 23:1–25)? The internalization of "The Law" is, readers recognize, a biblical theme of long standing (compare also Jer 4:3–4; 31:31–34; and Deut 29:1–3).

Planting of a New Heaven and a New Earth (51:9–16)

Who are "Rahab" and "Dragon," "Sea" and "the Great Deep"? The (near) identity of the last term to the name of the as yet unordered, "chaotic" deep of Gen 1:2 shows that mythic creation motifs provide the prophet-visionary with the cosmic imagery which sets the Lord's new creation into its scriptural frame of reference.

The preacher observes also that heaven and earth are portrayed as "perishable" (6) as well as capable of being "planted" anew (16). The cosmic motif is employed elsewhere in the book, too. Thus, the prologue appeals to "heaven and earth" as witnesses for the Lord's suit against the erring children of Israel (1:2), while the epilogue announces the coming into being of "a new heaven and a new earth" (66:22)—a telling correspondence between the book's beginning and conclusion (see the introductory discussion of the function of guide- and framewords).

A sermon may deal with the way in which biblical writings picture anticipated divine interventions as patterned by the Lord's action of old, hence the appeal in 51:9–16 to (mythically expressed) creation traditions. Do they not supply concept as well as warrant for the Lord's action in present and future (compare already Gen 9:1–17)? Noteworthy also is the manner in which the scriptural (re-)creation texts locate the center of the new genesis in a gardenlike enclosure, in which delight and joy reign supreme. In this passage Zion is refounded as the spiritual center for the dispersed descendants of Abraham, Isaac, and Jacob; it is "like Eden" (51:3). There is ample evidence in Scripture that the concept of the Temple and its city as tangible token of the divine presence, in its own way pictured earlier in the Paradise story, informs many a text (see Exod 40:33–35; 1 Kings 8:10–12; and compare Deut 12:8–12; Dan 6:11; but note also Rev 21:22–27).

However, any tangible token of the Lord's presence is and remains a symbol. It points the faithful to the manifestation of the divine as much as it denys any ultimate significance for itself. Voices of protest are raised already in Scripture when the Temple in Jerusalem is credited with greater dignity than appropriate. One is heard already in the book's epilogue (66:1–2; compare 1 Kings 8:12). Synagogue and Church know that other symbols, such as sacred office or holy season, are similarly metaphoric in nature.

The Arousal of Zion (51:17—52:6)

Twice Jerusalem is urged to rouse herself (51:17; 52:1), and her past humiliation is described in stark images (51:19–20; 52:1c–2a). The first extended paragraph of the text is dominated by the image of "the Lord's cup of reeling" (51:17, 22)—figurative expression for the accumulation of evils which have befallen the city: wreckage and ruin, famine and sword (19b). Jerusalem has had to drink the cup of wrath down to its bottom, but now that bitter fate is that of her tormentors (22–23).

Preachers know that the notion "cup" is familiar from the assurance of Ps 23 that those whose shepherd is the Lord find that their "cup runneth over"—for centuries a memorable image of well-being and blessing. On the other hand, Jer 26:15–29 paints a harsh picture of the Lord's making all nations drink from the cup of wrath; "Let them drink and retch and act crazy, because of the sword I am sending among them." The disquieting imagery is born, it must be noted, of the prophetic persuasion that all that happens on the world's stage is and can only be the work of Israel's God. The Lord is not only "first and last," but also the one who creates "light and darkness, weal and woe" (Isa 45:7; and note further comments on 45:1–8).

A sermon may also deal with Zion's anticipation that in the future "no uncircumcised and no unclean person" shall enter "the holy city." Then she will proudly wear "the robes of majesty" (52:1–2). Here the preacher recognizes that the visionary does not assume the abrogation of either the Abrahamic covenant or the Law of Moses. Circumcision, both of the flesh and in the heart, remains a mark also of renewed Israel (Gen 17:1–26; Jer 4:3–4; compare Deut 29:1–3 and Jer 31:31–34), as does the observance of ritual purity, outwardly as well as inwardly (Lev 19:1; 20:7–8; Isa 1:10–17; Hos 6:6). Most writings in the Hebrew Scriptures in principle set forth that view. However, in later periods Jewish and especially Christian groups began to debate the extent and the nature of the observation of the law of Moses, as well as its mediation "through angels." These discussions led, as must be expected, to tension and separation (compare Rom 10:4; Gal 3:1—4:31; but also Matt 5:17–19 and 22:34–40).

The Price of Redemption (52:7—53:12)

Here joyful acknowledgment of the good news announced to Zion, there contrite insight into the servant's suffering; here exuberant call to depart from a house of bondage, there description of a burial among strangers. The passage captures both the height and the depth of a people's journey through time and space, both the agony and the promise of its servanthood. It moves from the triumphal proclamation of the Lord's renewed accession to royal rule, visible to all creation, to the order given to the captives to leave behind their bars (52:7–10). The text then presents, in a sustained composition, the recognition, description, and confirmation of the servant's redemptive role (52:13—53:12).

A Greater Exodus (52:7–12)

The brief unit is cast as a reflection. It perceives, in visionary stance, "on the mountains the feet of one who brings good news" to the city which is now given a new lease on life. The returnees, it seems, are here portrayed as the first who break the news to Jerusalem and who assure her that "your God reigns as king." In this manner the paragraph summarizes what Isa 40—55 spells out in a variety of ways.

A sermon may fasten on the (doubled) occurrence of the word "announcer of (good) news"—the very term which in Isaiah and then in the NT refers to persons who are privileged to make known a decisive change of affairs which affects the addressees (see 40:9; 41:27; 66:1; as well as Mark 1:14 and Luke 4:16–21).

The preacher then notes that the call to leave Babylon, short and urgent, is formulated so as to evoke memories of the Exodus from Egypt. The contrast, however, is evident: the Israelites under Moses left Egypt "in haste" and, as it were, "in flight," but the émigrés from Babylon will not be under such duress (compare Exod 12:11, 33–36). Moreover, their forebears of old were guided only by a cloud by day and a fiery pillar by night, but now the Lord is both leading and following them so that they are safe (compare Exod 13:21–22). Finally, Israel of old had to carry its kneading bowls filled with dough; their latter-day descendants transport nothing less than the Lord's vessels, careful to touch nothing ritually impure as they proceed home (compare Exod 12:34; as well as 2 Kings 25:14–15 and Ezra 1:7–11).

The Cost of Servanthood (52:13—53:12)

The change in mood is striking. The divine voice draws the audience's attention to "my servant," the remnant people commissioned to restore not only Israel, but also their kinsfolk descended from Abraham and Sarah, Isaac and Rebekah (see 49:6).

Preview-like, the servant's humiliation and vindication are sketched in 13–15 with a few strokes. Then those to whom the servant's mandate is directed speak up (53:1–11a). They reflect on the insight which the servant's fate presses upon them. It is this: the misery and the derision which the faithful remnant had to endure—from deportation to acceptance of exile, from receiving the mandate to its execution—bring them, the curious bystanders, a new lease on life. Nothing less than a reversal has taken place: "The chastisement that makes us well, is laid upon him"—and not us (5b)! Now they recognize that the God of Israel is at work and conclude: "He shall rest content in his knowledge (of having done the Lord's bidding)" (11a). In confirmation the prophet gives the final word to the Lord (11b–12), and that speaks of the servant's vicarious suffering outright.

Aware that this text deals with one of the deepest mysteries encountered in life, that of violent and extreme but innocent suffering, the preacher may wish to explore that notion. The text itself uses a variety of images. There is first the theme of the seeming insignificance of the sufferers, and of the spectators' lack of interest in what they witness. Then the bystanders' recognition of the servant's willing acceptance is described, as is their claim that the sufferers were stricken by God. Finally, the insight rises within the spectators that it is their own fates that are at stake. Now they perceive the true nature of what they witness and so have to confess that they are the ones who have gone astray "like sheep." As bystanders turned beneficiaries, they affirm that the servant's mission has succeeded.

A sermon may reflect on the theme of redemptive suffering. Several of its biblical perspectives appear, because the text draws on a variety of its manifestations in Scripture. There is the story of Moses who, together with Aaron, Joshua, and Caleb, is in danger of being stoned by the Israelites when he remonstrates with them concerning their fearful response to the spies' reports and their lack of trust in Israel's God (see Num 14:10; also 13:1—14:45; Exod 2:11–15 and 15:22–25). Israel's opposition to several prophets is another example. Readers recall that the Lord interprets the people's desire for a king as rejection of Samuel (1 Sam 8:8), that Queen Jezebel threatens to kill Elijah after his successful ordeal on Mount Carmel (1 Kings 19:1–2), and that the king of Samaria vows to have Elisha's head taken off after the prophet has been unable, in the monarch's judgment, to avert siege and famine (2 Kings 6:31). Jeremiah would have perished in a cistern had not a courageous Ethiopian court official interceded for him (Jer 38:1–13; see also 26:1–19).

At least once the fate of a prophet of the Lord was outright martyrdom: Uriah had spoken the same message of doom to Jerusalem as Jeremiah; as a result King Jehoiakim had him put to death and buried without honor (Jer 26:20–23; compare Isa 53:9a). These texts are reflected in various aspects of the servant's suffering presented in 53:1–11a. Moreover, does the story of Abraham's (near) sacrifice of Isaac (Gen 22:1–19) not portray the patriarch's perfect obedience, and that at the price of his only heir's untimely death, a degree of suffering not unlike that of the servant?

Finally, we note that vicarious suffering has remained a painful issue ever since the Hebrew Scriptures have reflected upon it. The stories about ancient and modern martyrs bear ample testimony. For instance, in the narrative of the death of the mother and her seven sons in 2 Maccabees, the youngest of the brothers utters these last words, "I, like my brothers, give up body and life for the laws of our fathers, appealing to God to show mercy soon to our nation ... and ... to bring to an end the wrath of the Almighty which has justly fallen on our whole nation" (7:37–38 [1–41]; compare Isa 53:5–6). In a similar manner, followers of Jesus saw his innocent and violent death on a Roman cross as a martyrdom which was "a ransom for many" (Mark 10:45; compare John 10:7–15; 1 Tim 2:5–6), not to mention the author of Luke-Acts, who in this connection specifically refers to Isa 53:7–8 (Acts 8:26–40).

The Eternal Sign of Peace (54:1—55:13)

Like the final movement of a symphony, this passage brings the book's third part to its conclusion by drawing its major themes together. The mood is festive, the sentiments strong, the arguments persuasive, and the images forceful. The covenant theme is central and appears twice, once with reference to the covenant with Noah and once to that granted to David's house. Thus, one of the important features of the divine-human encounter as presented in "The Law and the Prophets" is evoked in order to bring to a climax the third part of the book.

The Assurance of Peace (54:1–17)

The by now familiar theme of Jerusalem's restoration to a position of importance and honor greater than before is illustrated not only with the pastoral image of a tent which its family has outgrown, but also with the assurance that the holy city will be surrounded by flourishing towns, the cities of Judah (1-3; compare 40:9-11). Again Jerusalem is comforted, this time also with the divine assertion that "for a short moment I have deserted you, but now I am gathering you in with great mercy" (7; compare 8). A reference to "the waters of Noah" (Gen 6:5—9:17) further supports the message: not only was that flood of desolation transitory, but its termination became the setting for the divine promise never to bring such a destruction again over the earth.

The preacher notes the manner in which the use of a scriptural narrative sets into broader perspective what at the moment may seem a crushing and enduring reality: Jerusalem in ruin for the span of almost two generations (587-538 B.C.E.). Though lasting much longer than the great flood of old, it will nevertheless come to an end. In fact, in the eyes of the God of Israel it is of only brief duration, terminated forever by divine compassion. Moreover, in keeping with the scriptural paradigm, the covenant theme brings the paragraph to its consoling climax: "My loyalty will not desert you nor my covenant of peace move from you" (10). Are not prosperity, blessing, and the absence of threat and strife gifts of Israel's God to the people of the Lord's inheritance (Exod 20:6; Deut 7:9; Num 6:24-26; Deut 28:1-14; Isa 57:19)?

Sapphires and rubies will secure the foundations of the restored city (11-12). The intriguing motif also appears elsewhere in the Scriptures. Thus, the high-priestly breastpiece of judgment is studded with twelve precious stones (Exod 28:15-21), and the King of Tyre, pictured in Ezekiel as primal man in the Garden of God, is similarly adorned (Ezek 28:13). By the same token, the heavenly Jerusalem shown to the seer on Patmos is set in jewels (Rev 21:15-21). The motif cannot but highlight the poetic exuberance of the last paragraphs of the book's third part. Readers note how their language "soars"—is this not the verbal image which describes at the beginning of that part (40:31) what trust in Israel's God accomplishes?

The Assurance of Permanence (55:1-13)

More than ten imperatives follow each other quickly but then give way to almost as many reasoning appeals, introduced by the conjunction "because." Those who are thirsty are invited to come to the water that satisfies, and those without means are invited to make purchases "without silver" and buy "wine and milk" without having to pay the price. Why expend good value for what does not offer nurture (1–2)? Evidently the addressees are beckoned in figurative language to come into the Lord's presence as found in the holy city; there an eternal covenant after the manner of the one granted to David and his house (2 Sam 7:8–16; Ps 89:20–38) will be made with them. Permanence marked that ancient divine promise, and now it is both affirmed and extended to all for whom Zion becomes home or pilgrimage center.

This observation shows the preacher once again the broadening of scriptural patterns which characterizes much of Isa 40—55 and 56—66. Thus, the departure from Babylon is like that from Egypt long ago but exceeds it in that the émigrés are not forced to be "in haste" (see the comments above on 52:7–12 and 43:16–21). The prophetic passages not only heighten scriptural motifs, but also seek through them to conceive the new which the Lord is doing in their time and place (see 43:19 and 42:10). Here the enduring nature of the divine re-creation comes into view—a notion welcomed by a people for whom the ups and downs of history have brought disruption, destruction, and deportation more than once or twice.

The assurance of permanence is coupled, however, with the provision that if any one of David's descendants fails to live according to the divine will, the Lord will discipline, though never abandon him: "I will be a father to him . . . When he does wrong, I will chastise him . . . but I will never withdraw my favor from him . . ." (2 Sam 7:14–15). Echoing that assurance, 55:3 speaks of the Lord's eternal covenant with the servant people, marked by both mercy and discipline. As unconditional promise, such covenant stands in tension with a conditional understanding of divine-human relationships. Thus, when Israel stands at Mount Sinai, it is told: "Now then, if you will obey me faithfully and keep my covenant, you shall be my treasured possession among all the peoples" (Exod 19:5).

Readers of the Jewish and Christian Scriptures know that the two covenant concepts have at times generated ambiguity, if not outright tension. Does the conditional understanding not assume (or at least imply) that the people's failure to obey the divine will cancels the covenantal relationship? Some prophetic voices seem to hold that view, though they are also quick to project a renewed (or is it a new?) covenant (compare Jer 31:31–34; 32:36–41; Hos 2:16–25). Writings of the NT reflect the tension in their own way: is Jesus' martyrdom the sealing of "a new covenant" or the renewal of the covenantal relationships which "The Law and the Prophets" attest (compare 2 Cor 3:6; Luke 22:20; and Heb 9:15 with Matt 5:17–19 and John 1:45)?

A sermon may explore the urgent and pleading invitation with which the book's third part concludes: "Seek the Lord while he may be found . . ." (6–9; compare 10–11). Preachers note that "the evildoer" and "the person concerned with nothingness" are addressed. What is the meaning of these seemingly self-evident terms? Their moral connotation, usually stressed and expressed by a word such as "sinners," needs to be set into a broader perspective. These terms are religious, even theological, in character. They refer to what may be called heterodox members of Israel, to those who practice forms of piety and observance which vary from those advocated in the texts (compare the comments on "images," 44:6–20 and 48:5). Thus, these concluding pleas are designed to change the minds of the addressees so that they adopt a different, deeper, and more comprehensive concept of divine presence in Israel and beyond its borders.

Is it not the prophet's mandate, given of old, in due time to open blind eyes and illumine darkened minds (6:9–13; 8:16–18; 35:5; 42:18–25)? Broadly speaking, the Book of Isaiah emphasizes that the new which it sets forth needs to be recognized, acknowledged, and internalized. The paragraphs of 55:1–11 plead for such a reconceptualization of Israel's God. To be sure, the element of the numinous and transcendent ultimately defies objectification—divine thoughts will remain as high above human comprehension as the heaven is high above the earth! Nevertheless, the prophetic mission is vindicated by the fulfillment of the Lord's word once spoken, and the book itself offers the evidence. The word of the Lord shall remain forever (40:6–8), and that word of Zion's greatness will be a sign "never to be cut off" (13).

Epilogue:
The Presence of Zion's Future
(Isaiah 56:1—66:24)

The epilogue corresponds to the prologue in that it celebrates what the latter anticipates. The first section (56:1—60:22) portrays the rise of Jerusalem to prominence in an unexpected manner: through her welcome to pilgrims and settlers alike, whether descendants of Jacob or Israel's kin through Abraham and Isaac, whether newly won, formerly excluded, or otherwise disadvantaged. The second section (61:1—66:24) presents Zion as the center of renewed Israel, the Lord's vineyard.

The Ascent of the Lord's City (56:1—60:22)

The compositional pattern which characterizes Isaiah in its entirety also appears here. Thus the thematic sequence broadly moves from threats to Israel's existence as people of the Lord to the human acknowledgment of these dangers, and concludes with divine affirmations of a full life for Israel and the Lord's city. A central note is struck early in the section: all are invited to the sanctuary on Mount Zion; is it not "a house of prayer for all nations" (56:7)?

The Lord's Peace for the Far and the Near (56:1—57:21)

Two thematically related units make up this passage. Both deal with the welcome which is to be accorded members of disadvantaged communities: proselytes and sterile persons on the one hand, and those despondent and depressed in spirit on the other.

Emancipation of the Disenfranchised (56:1–6)

Equal status for the proselyte and the sterile person is the theme. The text begins with a beatitude, then praises those who keep the Lord's law by hallowing the sabbath and by refraining from prohibited activity on that day (see Exod 20:8–11). The passage specifically directs itself to the two classes of observant but despondent people already noted. Proselytes cannot claim descent from Israel's father Jacob (Gen 29:31—30:24 and 35:16–18; compare 49:1–33). Barren persons, on the other hand, are without the prospect of family, that institution within society through which one's God-given inheritance is claimed and held (compare Gen 30:1–2 for an illustration of the despair of the barren wife). The text assures both of place and honor in renewed Israel.

Several words and motifs are noteworthy. Observance of the Lord's law is the appropriate mode of entrance into the presence of the divine. Thus, the keeping of the sabbath as "sign of the (Sinai) Covenant" (Exod 31:17) is the regularly renewed, visible symbol of devotion to the God of Israel (compare also 66:1–6). "Foreigners" may not be able to claim even Abraham as "father"—all the more reason to appeal to the Lord as "father" (see 63:16, 64:7). As those who voluntarily "come to" Israel, they are called "proselytes," a loanword from Greek expressing the notion of "coming to." "Eunuchs" are males who are infertile from birth or have been sterilized and are hence unable to found a family and so establish a future for themselves. This makes them especially suitable for offices of trust at royal courts (compare 39:7). The "barren" are promised a memorial, literally "hand and name," which is better even than physical descendants; the proselytes, on the other hand, are assured of acceptance as pilgrims and settlers in Jerusalem.

The preacher notes that the text counteracts the more restrictive view of lawgivers: while the exclusion of foreigners is not a hard-and-fast rule, that of sterile males is (Deut 23:2; contrast 23:3–8). Evidently the tension between prophetic vision beyond what obtains in the present and institutional interest in the preservation of the status quo is present already in the Scriptures—or rather, it continues in the life of Synagogue and Church today precisely because it is a biblical legacy. A sermon will seek to commend an inclusive attitude and to prepare the way for the reception of those not welcomed before—are they not also created in the image of God?

Inspiration for the Despondent (56:7—57:21)

The text deals with assurance to the depressed in spirit. It begins with the prophet's invitation to wild animals, urging them to come and ravage freely because the watchdogs are careless (56:9–12). Then it moves to the resigned observation that due to the irresponsible behavior of the people's leaders, those loyal to the Lord have lost heart (57:1–2). A stern condemnation of some seven kinds of apostasy follows (57:3–13), contrasted with calls to make ready the pilgrims' road for those who seek refuge on the Lord's mountain (57:14). The passage concludes with a divine assurance of well-being for the faithful, whether they live far or near (57:15–21).

The preacher observes that this text plays a special role within its wider contexts. Together with the welcome to the proselyte and the stranger (56:1–8), it emphasizes the Lord's turning to persons deprived of comfort through no fault of their own (56:1—57:21). The following section (58:1—59:21) will deal with persons who are indeed to be blamed, but who in contrition overcome their separation from the divine presence. Both sections conclude with the Lord's invitation to deprived and contrite alike, pointing to the restored and now hospitable holy city as that place from which light radiates (60:1–22; compare 2:2–4/5; 4:2–6; 35:1–10).

A meditative style is employed to set forth the visionary perspective. It allows the prophet to address different though related audiences, to quote the Lord or others, as well as to discourse on the topics raised. The reflective mode also permits the author to set literal and figurative formulations side by side (compare 57:9–11 with 12) or to voice ironic and derisive sentiments (57:11, 13).

The first paragraph (57:9–12) employs metaphors to describe those in charge as deaf, sleepy, and greedy guard dogs, and those who trouble the Lord's people as predators. Figure of speech then gives way to literal quotation of the bragging glutton. In short, the leaders' failure has almost eliminated individuals devoutly holding to the Lord (57:1–2; compare 1:10–20; 3:1–15; 32:1–8). Were it not for a remnant, all hope would be lost (compare 1:2–9; 37:30–32; 46:3–4).

The reprimand of the sorceress' offspring (57:3–13) proceeds to list in detail the apostasies of which inhabitants of Jerusalem are guilty. The idolatries mentioned call to mind comparable references (1:29–31; 65:3–5, 11–12; 66:3–4, 15–17; compare Exod 20:4–6; Jer 10:1–16; Ezek 8:1–18). Some of the rites listed in 5–9 cannot be identified with certainty. It seems that the following practices are censured: public fertility rites, infant dedications to Molech, offerings on (or to) stone pillars, sacrifices in mountain shrines, private setting up of images, idolatrous sexual practices in houses, and inquiry of the shades residing in the underworld. Their futility is beyond doubt, and their eventual disappearance certain (compare 44:6–20). On the other hand, life in the land of promise and festal celebration on its holy mountain are assured to those who make Zion the center of their devotion.

A sermon may deal with the topic of hospitality and focus on the prophet's order to prepare Jerusalem for the welcome of those who arrive after long travel (57:14). The reception of pilgrims and of new settlers calls for both physical arrangements and mental readiness. Those who may become discouraged by the crush of pilgrim crowds or the difficulties of resettlement are assured of divine support in spite of what seems to be evidence of the Lord's anger (compare 26:20; 51:7–8). Thus the doubled affirmation of well-being and peace as gifts to both "the far and the near" is metaphoric as well as factual: it addresses those who are distant from the divine presence either because they live far away (compare 42:1–4; 60:8–9; 66:18–20) or because they are still caught up in apostasy but ready to abandon it (compare 55:6–9; 65:8-10).

Preachers note the geographical as well as religious inclusiveness of the texts. Human beings who are broken in spirit, pained in body, or disenfranchised in society are sought and supported by the religious community. It will speak words of welcome, comfort, and new beginnings and will not permit fences to be erected where divine compassion makes no distinctions. NT discourses on Jesus' bringing reconciliation and peace to "those who are far and those who are near" (Eph. 2:11–22), as well as references to the restlessness of the disloyal, "tossed to and fro" like waves (Eph. 4:14; compare Jude 13), are also commentary on the passage.

The Lord's Acceptance of the Contrite (58:1—59:21)

This text also may be divided into two related passages. The first deals with the reward of hospitality for those who freely offer it, the second with the continuing prophetic challenge to extend welcome to those who turn to the Lord.

Rewards of Hospitality (58:1–14)

The passage decries exploitive actions toward pilgrims and settlers but also offers a divine promise of prosperity as result of receiving the visitor and observing the sabbath. This theme is unfolded in detail: first the prophet, summoned to announce to the Lord's people their disloyalty (1–2), quotes the people's indignant question directed to the Lord as to why their fasting remains unheeded (3a). The divine response relayed through the prophet (3b–14) rejects the cultic rites carried out by the Jerusalemites and demands instead tangible assistance to visitors and debt remission for needy settlers. Once such acts of charity are followed and confirmed by wholehearted sabbath observance, the Lord's people will be granted prosperity in the land inherited from their fathers.

Preachers may wish to deal with the theme of hospitality. It is, after the welcome extended to the proselyte and the eunuch (56:1–8) and the divine assurance for the despondent (56:9—57:21), yet another endorsement of the Temple in Jerusalem as "a house of prayer for all nations" (56:7; compare 2:2–4/5; 66:18–24, also Mark 11:15–17). Hence the passage is followed by an announcement of divine intervention on behalf of those who turn to the Lord (59:1–21) and by the account of the worldwide surge of peoples and nations toward the light that radiates from Mount Zion (60:1–22). The commendation of hospitality has remained for Judaism and Christianity one of the symbols of mutual acceptance and of the world-embracing nature of the two sister communions (see Heb 13:2 with reference to Gen 18:1–33; and Babylonian Talmud, Sabbath 127a: "Great is hospitality; greater even than early attendance at the House of Study or than the reception of the Heavenly Presence").

On the other hand, a sermon may explore the two kinds of ritual observance discussed: fasting and sabbath. The chastised inhabitants of Jerusalem observe both (3b–5, 13) but do so selectively in terms of the Law of Moses: they do indeed carry out what the regulations enjoin, but fail to abstain from what they prohibit. Ritual fasting, especially as practiced on the Day of Atonement, and the keeping of the holy day must be accompanied by abstention from every kind of work, not to mention gainful enterprises (Lev 16:29; Exod 20:8–11).

Moreover, the laws binding those who are loyal to the Lord prescribe charitable acts for the benefit of those without means of support, notably strangers and the poor (Exod 22:20, 24).

Some of the descriptions of unacceptable actions are not altogether clear. They seem to belong to two groups. One relates to the enslavement of a fellow Israelite for unpaid debts (6, 9b), which the Law limits to a six-year period (Exod 21:2–11). The other relates to the supply of food, shelter, and clothing to indigent members of one's larger family (7, 10a). The preacher also notes the various phrases (8–9a, 10b–12) describing the city's future well-being; this evidently is contingent on its full observance of the Lord's law. That condition does not (yet) prevail; the city and its sanctuary are only beginning to grow toward their future greatness (compare Hag 2:3). On the other hand, many verbal images here and elsewhere celebrate the imminence of the city's glorious future (see 51:1–3; 59:15–20; 60:1–3, 10–14).

Finally, a sermon may focus on the apparent rejection of the performance of outward, visible, and tangible rites and their replacement by inward and secret attitude (compare, for example, Matt 6:16–18). However, the prophetic word is directed against selective obedience, condemned also in the prologue (1:10–20). If only some of the demands of religion are accepted while others are in principle ignored, piety is in danger of becoming hypocrisy. Then stern words are in order: "I can no more endure apostate action alongside solemn assembly!" (1:13). The whole of human existence is laid under the divine claim. In the new situation prevailing after the Edict of King Cyrus (45:13; 2 Chron 36:23), the role of Jerusalem as host city of pilgrims and center of returnee-settlers demands of its residents, priest, Levite, and layperson alike, the exercise of hospitality on a scale unknown before. Have not many newcomers arrived with more love of Zion in their hearts than money in their purses?

Permanence of Obligation (59:1–21)

The theme is the continuance of the prophetic challenge presented in 58:1–14 specifically and in Isa 1—66 generally. The first two verses are a preview of the text: the people's separation from the divine presence is due not to the Lord's weakness, but to its apostasy. The text then unfolds the thesis and does so in the form of a liturgy. The full account of the people's acts of disloyalty (3–8) is followed by the addressees' confession of these very deeds (9–15a). The description of the expected divine intervention for Jacob's descendants who turn from apostasy (15b–20) is the response to the people's admission, concluded by the prophet's quotation of the Lord's assurance that prophetic challenges such as this one will accompany Israel into the future (21).

The meditative style, already noted in compositionally similar texts (for example, 56:9—57:21), allows the author to move freely into summary proposition (1–2) or detailed description (3–8, 15b–20), into the quotation of the people's confession (9–15a) or of a divine affirmation (21). Moreover, the reflective mood favors the use of similes, whether drawn from the animal world (5–6a, 11a), from the sphere of physical handicaps (10a), from that of military equipment (17), or from geography (19).

Preachers observe that the passage plays a double role in the wider context of "The Ascent of the Lord's City" (56:1—60:22). On the one hand, it brings to a climax the castigations directed against narrow-minded members of the Lord's people, that is, those who exclude proselyte and eunuch (56:1–8), those who pay no heed to persons loyal to the Lord (56:9—57:21), and those who fail to offer hospitality and remission of debts (58:1–14). These acts of disloyalty are cited in the people's liturgical confession which the prophet quotes (59:9–15a). On the other hand, the passage leads to the invitation to enjoy Zion's radiance, which is nothing less than a complete reversal of its former state (60:15–22; compare 59:15b–18, 20a).

Several phrases call for comment. The opening statement is a double negation. It emphatically denies the claim that the Lord is too frail to intervene. This argument is also rejected in the paragraph which deals with the notion that the Lord has divorced his people (50:1–3). Evidently this was a weighty challenge and needed to be dismissed at the outset. Does not that earlier text emphatically formulate the question of Israel's God: "Is my hand shortened that it cannot redeem? Or have I no power to deliver?" (50:20).

A sermon may also deal with the many words referring to

the people's apostasy or to the loyalty demanded of them: iniquity, sin, crime, falsehood, treachery, evil on the one hand, and integrity, justice, honesty, uprightness, good on the other. Each of these two word groups is made up of near synonyms; the words are interchangeable and refer to the same attitude and activity. Contrary to the impression they make on first sight, they are primarily religious-theological, not moral-ethical, in nature. In other words, they refer to sentiments, words, and actions which issue from the spirit of loyalty (or disloyalty) to the Lord and the Law of Moses. To be sure, in many cases the positive and negative manifestations of such attitudes have moral-ethical significance and are praiseworthy or are to be condemned. However, biblical writings employ these terms generally to describe aspects of observance or nonobservance (compare Josh 23:6, 2 Kings 23:25; Ps 1:2), hence they are in this preaching guide usually rendered by synonyms or antonyms of "loyalty (to the Lord and the Law of Moses)." This insight mitigates the tendency of Western Christianity toward a moralizing understanding of these biblical words and toward a primarily ethical conception of its religious tradition. Furthermore, the word choices of modern translations reinforce this tendency, not to mention the common understanding of such a basic part of the liturgy as the "Confession of Sin." In short, Scripture usually condemns spiritual wrongheadedness rather than moral evil-mindedness.

The description of the divine intervention (15b–20) presents it as brought on by the failure of those who should be the people's mainstays: its rulers and counselors, its priests and prophets (15b–16a; compare 1:21–23; 3:1–15; 28:7–13; 29:9–14; 56:10–12). Hence it is the Lord's "loyalty" to the people which initiates the divine intervention (16b). The Lord is figuratively described as "warrior," hence words like divine "helmet, armor, and coat" appear (17; compare Eph 6:14, 17; I Thess 5:8). The dominant theme is that of the responsibility of persons appointed to office and their accountability to both Israel's God and the people whom they are called to serve.

A sermon may deal with the divine affirmation of a solemnly initiated, "covenanted" relation of the Lord with the people, mediated in perpetuity by prophets who follow in the footsteps of Isaiah (21; compare 8:16–18; 48:16b). The text points to the prophet's spirit-empowered announcement of the Lord's favor (61:1–3). It also builds on a preceding passage according to which the prophet speaks of himself as one who stands at the start of a line of successors. According to 8:11–23a, Isaiah is ordered by the Lord "to bind up testimony and to seal it among my disciples." The man of God then affirms that "I and the disciples (literally: children) whom the Lord gave me, are signs and portents in Israel." As those who alone and exclusively grasp their master's "vision of the whole" (29:1–12; compare 6:1–13), they begin the succession of prophets of the Lord primarily represented by them, by Jeremiah and (his successor) Ezekiel, and also by Haggai and Zechariah (Jer 15:15–17; Ezek 2:8–10; Hag 1:1; Zech 1:1). In other words, 59:21 and its related texts present a warrant for the composition of the Book of Isaiah and of the prophetic books which follow (Jeremiah–Malachi). Contemporary preaching, though primarily empowered by the NT call to reconciliation and the new life in Christ Jesus which it offers, will seek to locate itself also in that earlier, prophetic succession by offering words both of discipline and of acceptance, of chastisement and of consolation.

The Invitation to Zion's Radiance (60:1–22)

The passage is one of the prophet's fullest summons for Jerusalem to rise and recognize that the day of her glory has dawned. The opening call (1–3), speaking of light and darkness, of the Lord's glory and of kings' arrival, sets forth in bold strokes what the following paragraphs lay out in detail.

First the city, rising from the ruins, is urged to realize what is happening in the spectacle of the pilgrims' and returnee-settlers' arrival in its gates. Not only are Jerusalem's sons and daughters coming back, but they are also bringing the wealth of their host countries by the camel-load. There are gold and incense from Midian, Ephah, and Shebah, choice sacrificial rams from Kedar, and precious metals from Tarshish (4–9). Secondly, Zion is told of a double marvel. The bounty brought to her makes possible the building of walls and gates which, as befits a pilgrim city, stand open day and night (10–12); moreover, the sanctuary, beautified by cedar and cypress woodwork, is visited with reverence even by those who once afflicted the city (13–14). Finally, Zion finds its humiliation completely reversed: instead of desertion there is the joy of hosting guests, common building materials are replaced by expensive ones, instead of victims' cry justice reigns, instead of sun and moon the Lord is the city's illumination, and even its smallest families become as populous as strong nations.

The choice of words and themes highlights the exaltation of Jerusalem, and the formulation of the individual paragraphs suggests the inclusiveness of the divine action. The geographical horizon is impressive: Mediterranean lands as far away as Tarshish (Sardinia or Spain) are in view, as are regions of Arabia to the East and South (9, 7). By the same token, high and low among the world-dispersed descendants of Jacob, Isaac, and Abraham are among the travelers: commoners as well as "kings" (compare 49:7; leading figures in diaspora communities?), including persons who once had opposed Jerusalem's claims and had "troubled" it (3, 10–11, 14). The pilgrims and the settlers come in families made up of mothers and fathers together with their offspring (compare Luke 2:41–51); all of them are summarily described as "sons and daughters of Zion" (4). Exhilaration also speaks through the explicit reference to tribes descended from Abraham (compare Gen 25:2, 4, 3, 13) and the identification of the Lord as "the Strong One of Jacob" (16; 1:4; see comment on 49:26 above). Thus, as set forth in 49:6, the mandate of the Lord's servant reaches beyond the twelve tribes of Jacob and seeks to bring together those who according to the Genesis story have become estranged (see comment on 49:6). Finally, the reversal of Zion's fate is described with no fewer than five different motifs (15–22).

Preachers note that the portrayal of the city's new splendor is that which characterizes a new creation; in fact, it will be described in this manner in 65:17–20 and 66:22–24. The observation explains why the Lord, rather than sun and moon, will be Jerusalem's light. Did not these celestial bodies serve as the lights of the "old" creation, only called into being three days after the appearance of the divine light on the first creation day (compare Gen 1:14–19 with 1:3–5)? By the same token, the upgrading of the city's building materials (17) not only corresponds to the precious stones into which its walls are set (54:11–12), but also compares favorably with what King Solomon did for the city (1 Kings 10:27). Moreover, the reign of justice and peace (18) contrasts with the failure to observe the Lord's law in the past (59:7; 1:21–23; 3:1–15; 30:9–11). Similarly, the free access to the city, even at night when gates are traditionally shut and barred (11), marks it as place of peaceful pilgrimage and not as fortress which has to expect attacks (7:1–9; 11:28–32; 36:1–3). Finally, the fecundity of its people, a result of their religious faithfulness (21–22), is illustrated by that of Abraham who had been "called when he was only one" (51:2).

A sermon may take its cue from the two guidewords "light" (1 [twice], 3, 19 [three times]) and "glory" (7 [twice], 9, 13, 19, 21). The use of guidewords in the composition of a passage, discussed in the Introduction, is a characteristic feature of Scripture. Thus, the notion of divinely supplied light begins one of the creation stories in Genesis (Gen 1:2—2:4a). Starkly contrasted with darkness (60:2; compare Gen 1:3–5), it is the dominant quality of the celestial, divine sphere. Its "rising" in the earthly realm (60:1, 2) alerts those who have been given eyes to see (compare 32:3, 35:5; 42:18–19; but also Mark 4:9, 23) that divine creativity is at work.

By the same token, the juxtaposition of this guideword with the other one, "glory," relates the radiance of the city to that of the Lord's presence in the Holy of Holies, the innermost part of the Temple. In other words, the God of Israel is found both within and without the human sphere, is both immanent and transcendent. The tokens of the divine presence, such as the Temple with its seasons of joy at the pilgrimage festivals, give human beings not control over but a share in the divine presence. Thus, Jerusalem is celebrated as "the city of our assemblies" (33:20) where intertribal rivalry and hostility are overcome and the Lord's instructions heeded, where strangers feast with each other as sons and daughters of Zion, and where sheltering canopy has replaced deserted hut (2:2–4; 54:1–3; 25:6–8; 4:2–6; compare Matt 8:5–13; John 12:30). In the words of Josephus, a Jewish historian of the first century C.E.: "Let the Israelites assemble in that city in which they shall establish the temple, three times in the year ... in order to give thanks to God, to pray for future acts of mercy, and to promote by meeting and feasting together feelings of mutual affection" (*Antiquities* IV 203).

The Center of Worldwide Israel (61:1—66:24)

After the epilogue's first part (56:1—60:22) has celebrated the rise of the holy city from ruin, obscurity, and exclusiveness to restoration, luster, and inclusiveness, its second part (61:1—66:24) describes Jerusalem's role as the visible spiritual center of Judaism. The servant-people's announcement of Israel's release into a new creation (61:1—63:6) finds its response in a liturgy of the renewed but still chastised vineyard (63:7—65:25); then the epilogue concludes the book with a final description and clarification of the divine presence in the holy city (66:1–24).

The Announcement of Israel's Liberation (61:1—63:6)

Here jubilant declaration, there rhetorical question; here doubled imperatives, there solemn oath—the passage is compositionally varied and stylistically full of life. First Israel's liberation is proclaimed as the work of that divine spirit which empowers the prophetic voice (61:1–11); then the new roles of Zion and its land as city of pilgrimage and divinely favored region are laid out (62:1–12); and finally the Lord's intervention against Israel's opponents is pictured in a memorable question and answer exchange (63:1–6).

Liberation Through the Spirit (61:1–11)

Now the hour of the servant-people has come: filled with the spirit of the Lord, the servant announces no fewer than five related aspects of the renewal (1–3). There is the good news of healing for the brokenhearted (1b), the message of release for those still forcibly detained (1c), the announcement of the new start which the jubilee year makes possible (2a), the comfort of all who lament Zion's fate (2b), and finally the appointment of Zion as "the Lord's planting" (3). Thus, the Israelites, their sanctuary in the process of being restored, become "priests of the Lord" (4–9), and the city sings of itself as vested with righteousness, adorned like bride and groom, and flourishing like a garden (10–11).

Preachers recognize several themes suitable for sermons. There is Luke's portrayal of Jesus' introduction of his mission in the synagogue of Nazareth (4:14–30). Luke's account moves from the quotation of 61:1–2 to the identification of two observant non-Israelites, the widow of Zarephat (1 Kings 17:8–24) and the Syrian officer Naaman (2 Kings 51:1–27), as representatives of the people addressed by Isaiah as well as by Jesus, and ends with the rejection of Jesus by the people in the house of worship. Here is a stern reminder that the inclusive view, advocated by servants of the Lord such as Luke's Jesus and Isaiah's servant, demands a high price. Acceptance of the outcast not only is commended at the beginning of the epilogue (56:1–8, 9–57:21), but is also the theme of programmatic paragraphs in the prologue (2:1–4/5; 4:2–6). There can be little doubt that in the development of Synagogue and Church the tension between inclusiveness and exclusiveness, between universalism and particularism, has surfaced time and again; in Christian communities it has led to strong affirmations of the worldwide horizons of the presence of the God of Israel (compare, for example, Matt 28:16–20; John 17:20–26; and Rom 3:29).

On the other hand, the notion that renewed Israel will be called not only "priests of the Lord" (compare 62:12) but also "those who render personal service to our God" (6a) reminds the audience of two different, though related, scriptural appointments to service. The people of Israel, encamped at the foot of Mount Sinai, is told that its obedience will prompt the Lord to make it "a holy nation" and "a kingdom of priests" (Exod 19:6). By the same token the prophet Elisha, after accepting Elijah's call, leaves everything and follows his newly found master by "rendering personal service" to him (1 Kings 19:19–21). The two models of ministry, one of cultic office, the other of self-denial by a migrant charismatic, are echoed in early Christian writings (see 1 Peter 2:9–10 and Mark 1:16–20). Thus ritual and personal, communal and individual aspects of service are juxtaposed.

Finally, Zion speaks joyfully of her renewal, using three tangible comparisons (10–11): she is "vested with a cloak of righteousness," is "adorned like groom and bride" are at their festive day, and "sprouts like a planted garden." The suggestiveness of the images to audiences knowledgeable in the Scriptures (compare Isa 5:7; Hos 1–3; Gen 2:8–9) also points to their figurative dimensions. Most of all, it is the frameword "loyalty/righteousness/mutual love" which distinguishes the renewed city, and that in pointed contrast to its earlier fallen state (3:1–15, 16—4:1; compare 28:1–22).

Zion's New Role (62:1–12)

The prophet first considers his own role (1–5), then moves outward to the city of Jerusalem (6–9), and concludes with instructions to those who are in charge of services for pilgrims and newcomers, presumably lower clergy and gatekeepers (10–12). Several topics appeal to the preacher.

Twice the juxtaposed guidewords "husband" and "pleasure" appear in 1–5 (4b,c), followed by the repetition of words referring to "husband(ing)" (5). The two images portray both the Lord's rule over and love for the people—a combination found also in Hos 1–3, not to mention its use with reference to Christ and the Church (Eph 5:29–33). The interpreter recognizes both the limitation and the possibility presented by such metaphors—is not biblical language marked by both earthy concreteness and the openness toward the figurative dimension? Failure to recognize the latter not only confines the appropriation of scriptural themes, but also prevents their creative, free unfolding in a new time and a new place. Moreover, does not the opening line of the paragraph as well as an assertion made by Jeremiah (20:9) attest that the Lord's word does not allow itself to be contained within the one commissioned to speak it (compare also 1 Cor 9:16)?

The appeals to make the holy city ready for the reception of and extension of hospitality to its visitors, returnee-settlers and pilgrims alike (6–9, 10–12), deal with several measures. There is the stationing of watchmen on its walls, whose duty it is to remind those who are gathered within their precincts of the Lord's power and presence. They do so "all day and all night"—an exuberant formulation indeed! The city gates are open day and night and thus show that Jerusalem is no more a fortress fearing attack but a center of welcome expecting peaceful visitors (see further comments on 60:11 [1–22]). It follows that the resented requisitioning of food and drink by occupying armies gives way to enjoyable feasting on the Temple grounds, enjoyed by observant Israelite as well as non-Israelite, by pilgrim and resident alike (compare Deut 14:26 [22–29]).

Finally, a sermon may deal with the concrete aspects of the welcome to be offered to the comers (10–12). There is the grading of and removal of stone from the roadways leading to and through the city gates and the maze of houses between the walls and the Temple entrances. Furthermore, signs must be set up to mark the approach streets—it is this very word which identifies Jerusalem and its royal house as a "sign" to the peoples abroad (compare 11:12, 10 [10–16]). Indeed, Jerusalem has remained the pilgrimage center for the faithful within Judaism, and Christians visit it as well, mindful of the setting of Jesus' last teaching, passion, death, and resurrection (see Mark 11:1—16:8; John 11:55—20:29; and note especially Luke 13:33 [31–35]).

The Humiliation of the Nations (63:1–6)

A striking rhetorical question and answer exchange introduces the imagery of the Lord's "treading (nations) in a winepress" and "blood staining his vestments." Its formulations are noteworthy—have they not inspired the words of the well-known (North American) "Battle Hymn of the Republic"? Here also the preacher does well to emphasize the metaphorical qualities of many a biblical text and scriptural formulation.

This passage sets forth the insight that the Lord is all-powerful; whatever events occur and shape the fates of human beings, nations, and religious communities are the Lord's doing. Is God not the cause of all that is and comes into being? After all, it is the Lord who creates "weal and woe," "light as well as darkness" (45:7). The mention of Edom as the place whence Israel's God comes to the people and the city of election highlights once more (compare 34:5–17) the tension between Israel and Edom, a nation closely related by family ties (note the Jacob/Esau stories in Gen 25—36). It seems that at one time in the past, Edom similarly spoke with satisfaction of Judah's and Jerusalem's ruin and is accordingly chastised for the lack of brotherly compassion (see Obad 1–21).

Liturgy of a New Creation (63:7—65:25)

From Moses and the Exodus in the distant past to the Lord's future making of a new heaven and a new earth—the wide horizon gives to the stylistically varied passage conceptual unity. The sustained composition reminds the audience of communal laments such as Pss 74 and 79. Supplications for divine intervention are supported by rehearsals of the Lord's past actions on Israel's behalf (compare 63:7–14 with 63:15—64:11). What distinguishes this text, however, are its concluding proclamations of the anticipated greater and more excellent divine gifts (65:1–15). Like the preceding and following text units of the epilogue, the lively alternation of prophetic reflections, divine assurances, and communal responses give it a liturgy-like quality. It seems that this and similar texts both inspire and mirror collective observances and individual musings, prayers, and sermons of Israel in dispersion as it finds its new role of worldwide religious community in the wake of King Cyrus' edict in 538 B.C.E. (Ezra 1:2–4; compare 5–11). The text may be divided into three parts: rehearsal, supplication, and proclamation.

The Recital of the Lord's Guidance (63:7–14)

The prophetic voice speaks like that of a psalmist: the memory of the Lord's gracious acts is followed by the call to praise Israel's God (63:7), corresponding, as it were, to a compositional order evident in the Hebrew Bible at large. There "A Book of Remembrance" (so named in Mal 3:16 and identical with Genesis–Malachi as ordered in the Hebrew Scriptures ; see Introduction for details) is followed by the Psalter, the praises of Israel (see Ps 22:4 and Isa 60:6).

Several topics suggest exploration. For instance, there is the well-known notion that the Lord's people failed in their obedience yet were guided by their God and brought into the land of promise. Israel's God acted for the sake of the divine name and thus did not allow the people's disloyalty to frustrate the divine design. The emphasis on God's all-sufficiency counters the people's real or anticipated boasts that they owed life, prosperity, and blessing to their own strength or merit (compare 63:10a with 48:5 and Deut 8:8–11).

A sermon may also deal with the prophetic assertion that the Lord will, in extreme cases of the people's faithlessness, instead of intervening on their behalf, fight against them. This may occur through the instruments of divine anger, notably the world powers of Assyria and Babylonia (10:5–6; Jer 25:1–14), or even directly: "I myself will fight against you (King Zedekiah) with outstretched hand and strong arm, in anger, and in fury, and in great wrath" (Jer 21:5 [1–7]; compare Deut 26:8 [5–11], where the very same phrases are used to describe the Lord's opposition to Egypt!). Such texts are painful reminders that the God of Israel indeed works "weal and woe" (45:7).

The identification of God's "holy spirit" as the agent of divine action (63:10, 14) also merits the preacher's attention. More than once in Isa 1—66 it is the divine spirit through which the new is called into being. Thus the king after God's heart acts in accord with the divine spirit, manifesting wisdom and understanding, knowledge and strength, and most of all the fear of the Lord (11:2), as did Moses before him (63:11). On the other hand, the servant-people is empowered for its mission of liberation within and beyond the tribes of Israel through the gift of the Lord's spirit (42:1; 61:1; compare 48:16), and the sphere of those who trust in the Lord is not that "of flesh, but of the spirit" (31:3 [1–3]). Finally, the gift of the divine spirit for all members of God's people, already desired by Moses (Num 11:29 [10–34]), is what the composer of Acts announces (2:1–13).

Supplication for the Lord's Epiphany (63:15—64:11)

The liturgy's second part intrigues readers by its memorable (and, especially in 64:1–4, barely intelligible) imagery. Thus, the plea for a divine "rending of the heavens" is directed to a God who is—only here in Isaiah—called "our father." The description of Israel's apostate and desperate condition is countered by the rhetorically couched wish that its God appear suddenly and miraculously. The people's acknowledgment that they are but clay in their maker's hand is followed by their wistful remembrance of the glories of Solomon's Temple, in the light of which the evidently small beginnings of their rebuilding program pale into insignificance (compare 1 Kings 6:1—9:9 with Hag 2:1–9).

The preacher may wish to explore the notion of divine fatherhood. It appears in the Hebrew Scriptures only here and in the farewell speech with which King David, according to Chronicles, commends his son and successor Solomon to the Lord's favor (1 Chron 29:10[10–19]). Thus the triple occurrence of that phrase in 63:15—64:11 is as unusual as it is weighty. It is striking that this appeal to the Lord frames the assertion that "Abraham has not known us, nor does Israel (Jacob) recognize us." Is the Lord's "fatherhood" here claimed by proselytes who of course cannot claim physical descent from these "fathers" of Israel? Or is the inability of the latter to intercede on their descendants' behalf the point (compare Jer 15:1; Ezek 14:12–20)? At any rate, the appeal parallels the Lord's "fatherhood" with "creatorship" (64:7) and thus may suggest that proselytes who now include themselves in God's people derive their warrant from bearing the divine image (compare Gen 1:2—2:4a).

Whatever the force of the appellation, readers know that in early Christian texts claims to God's "fatherhood" are both important and controversial. Thus Jesus' claim that God is uniquely his "father" reassures him and his followers but also makes him in the eyes of others guilty of blasphemy (Mark 14:36 [32–42]; Matt 5:43–48; John 5:18 [2–47]; compare Matt 6:9 [7–15]; Rom 8:15 [12–17]). Moreover, contemporary preachers recognize that the biblical image of God as "father" reflects ancient society's patriarchal order. Thus, interpreters employing today's understanding welcome the emphasis on inclusiveness which is evident already in the Scriptures (compare, for example, 19:23–25; 49:6; Jer 1:4–10; also Gal 3:28 and Col 1:15–20) and seek to conceptualize the divine presence and activity in both male and female imagery.

Proclamation of a New Creation (65:1–25)

The liturgy ends with assurances spelled out with a clarity not heard before. First, the members of new Israel are promised a future of well-being and blessing, while those who "forsake the Lord" will have to endure shame and deprivation (1–10, 11–14). Then no fewer than four related symbols of the divine re-creation are presented: the granting of a different divine name, the establishment of a new heaven and a new earth, the securing of Jerusalem as a safe and secure planting, and finally, the assurance of prevenient grace (15–16, 17–18, 19–23, 24–25).

The preacher notes that even the renewed people of God are not without those who deny the Lord. Their idolatrous practices are enumerated (3–5) and likened to those of their forebears (7; compare 1 Kings 11:7 [6–8]; Jer 3:23 [21–25]; Ezek 6:13 [1–14]). Moreover, they "forget the Lord's holy hill" and make ritual offerings of food and drink to "Luck" and "Destiny," evidently divinities of fate (11). They are contrasted with "my servants," that is, persons who respond to the Lord's call to exclusive adherence to the Lord and to worship on Mount Zion; these will be privileged to enjoy food, drink, and festive song (13–14). Their despondency overcome, they will drink of the water of life (compare 55:1–3). In other words, they will be physically and spiritually sustained by their devotion to the Law and the Temple of the Lord, whether they reside in distant lands or in Canaan. By the same token, those who are disloyal will be disoriented, depressed, and broken in heart—just as Moses' farewell speech anticipated (compare 14b with Deut 28:65–67).

The four gifts of divine renewal exceed those given of old. Each of them may become the basis of a sermon or serve as illustration in a homily on God's power of recreating those who long for it.

There is first the granting of "another (divine) name," which will not only identify God's people in a new way but also provide the vehicle of oaths for those who reside in or visit the land of promise (15–16). The "other name" is actually given, and that twice. It is usually rendered "God of truth" because it combines the word for "God" with the interjection "amen," which is based on the notions of reliability, trustworthiness, firmness, truth. The combination is already grammatically puzzling. It is without parallel in Scripture (but see Rev 3:14). However, the disclosure of a different, new divine name to humans is the first point of the divine revelation to Moses, as told in Exodus 6:2–9. There he is told that the deity appearing to him is "the Lord." The divine voice then affirms, "I appeared to Abraham, Isaac, and Jacob as El Shaddai (RSV: God Almighty; so already the Septuagint), but I did not make myself known to them by my name Yahweh (Lord)." Evidently, here the new name incorporates and supersedes the earlier one (compare Gen 17:1–2). Does the "other name" of Isa 65:16 similarly transcend the one granted to Moses and Israel at the holy mountain in the wilderness? Just as the deliverance of old is marked by a new divine name, so the present and greater liberation of the captives is sealed by the new name of Israel's God. This observation, however, does not illumine the meaning of that name—contrary to what is told in Exod 3:13–14. While the notion of trust and truth, as suggested by "God of Amen," is a reasonable translation, one wonders whether the three Hebrew consonants veil a meaning no longer accessible to modern interpretation.

"A new heaven and a new earth"—such a phrase is not easily overlooked. It describes what the Lord is doing in the most comprehensive terms (17–18). Does not the brief reference to the creation story of Gen 1:2—2:4a, as given at the beginning of the other in Gen 2:4b, summarily speak of the Lord's making "of heaven and earth"? Moreover, the book's prologue begins with an appeal to "heaven and earth" (1:2), and its epilogue ends with the phrase, repeated and expanded by the telling qualification "new" (65:17; 66:22). In short, what is now happening through the Temple's restoration, the rebuilding of the city, and Israel's renewal, both abroad and in Canaan, is nothing less than the coming into being of a new heaven and a new earth. This transforms the old heaven and the old earth of Gen 1:2—2:4a in the same manner in which the new ingathering of the Lord's redeemed exceeds the old (11:10–13; 49:8–13; compare Jer 31:34; Ezek:1–14). Little wonder that early Christian texts again celebrate the re-creative action of Israel's God and speak outright of "a new creation" (2 Cor 5:17 [11–21]; Rev 21:1–2, 5; compare 2 Peter 3:13 [10–13]).

The third gift of renewal is Jerusalem's prosperity (19–23). Its re-creation is described in terms of the longevity and fertility of its people and of the security and success of its life. Such good things are foretaste of and warrant for the holy city's uninterrupted, regular worship, portrayed in the concluding part of the epilogue (66:22–23). Moreover, the renewed city is the center of the new creation which has just been announced. Thus, the sequence "new creation—new holy precinct" mirrors a similar sequence evident in the manner in which the second creation story may be read as introducing the center for the already created sphere. Does not the seer on the island of Patmos likewise perceive the coming down of the heavenly Jerusalem as both following and centering the new creation (Rev. 21:1–2)?

The last gift is the promise that the Lord will respond to the people's prayers even before they utter them (24–25). In other words, here the prevenience of the Lord's grace is affirmed. The prosperity of the new creation will be manifest not only in this new token of divine mercy, but also in the reconciliation of animals who until then were enemies (see comments on 11:1–9). Even the story of a snake's success in tempting Adam and Eve (Gen 3:1–24) is countered: on the Lord's holy mountain this creature shall no more pose danger but shall be satisfied with dust as its (provider of) food!

The Elusive Divine Presence (66:1–24)

Here the assurance of the Lord's presence on Jerusalem's holy mountain, there near ridicule of ritualists who take pride in the rebuilt Temple; here the description of the marvel of Zion giving birth before labor pains overtake her, there the gruesome picture of the apostates' corpses—the range of imagery is wide and the juxtaposition of themes stark. Through them the passage concludes the equally comprehensive composition of Isa 1—66 and portrays for the last time the Lord's elusive presence, of which the book speaks from beginning to end.

Moreover, also here announcements of the divine word alternate with statements addressing different groups of persons, and both are supported by prophetic reflections and explanations. Three smaller units may be identified: the encouragement for the students of the Lord's word (1–6), the reassurance for the "lovers of Zion" (7–14), and the promise of the permanence of Jerusalem as the center of worldwide Judaism (15–24).

The Supremacy of the Lord's Word (66:1–6)

Twice those who are "greatly concerned for (literally: tremble in relation to) the Lord's word" are addressed. They are "the (spiritually) poor and those of broken heart" who find themselves ridiculed by their "brothers." The tension within renewed Israel is evidently strong and pits, as it were, ritualists against those who internalize and ponder the divine utterances availabe to them.

A sermon may explore this clash and note the manner in which an external, almost mechanical reliance on the existence of a rebuilt holy building is condemned (see also Jer 7:1–15). The house of worship cannot contain the divine presence! Is not heaven the Lord's throne and the earth merely the footstool of the divine power? Does not the selective observance practiced by ritualists amount to disloyalty condemned already in 1:10–20? In this manner may be explained the puzzling juxtaposition of four commendable acts of devotion to the Lord and four acts issuing from apostasy in 66:3. Those who are reassured, on the other hand, are the persons for whom the book is written, the servant-people struggling to grasp the insight to which the book of Isaiah bears witness. Does not their meditation on the Lord's word (compare Ps 1:2, 19:7–14) lead them into the wide horizons of the divine plan and impart to them "a vision of the whole" (29:11; compare 28:23–29)? For and by such students writings portraying divine action are conceived, written, and transmitted, generating in due time compositions such as "The Law and the Prophets." They enable the faithful "to recognize the difference between those who are loyal to the Lord and those who are faithless, between those who serve Israel's God and those who do not" (Mal 3:18 [13–18]).

The Vindication of Jerusalem's Lovers (66:7–14)

Images of quick, painless birth, of crowding multitudes, and of surprising growth portray the reversal of the holy city's humiliation and its supporters' sadness. They are here called "lovers of Zion," highlighting the intimate devotion of those who are returnee-settlers or visitors in holy season.

A homily may explore the notion of the tangible center which Jerusalem has become for Judaism. The practice of pilgrimage, mandated of old in Moses' farewell speech (for example, Deut 16:1–17), is the common expression of that devotion, not to mention the desire of many an observant son and daughter of Jacob, Isaac, and Abraham to settle in the land of promise (see 2:1–4; 4:2–6; and 60:1–22 and the comments made there in relation to reassuring as well as limiting aspects of any identification of a holy site).

The Circle and the Center (66:15–24)

The comprehensive horizon with which the book begins, through its appeal to "heaven and earth" as witnesses against Israel (1:2), appears also at its conclusion. However, now that double phrase is qualified by the adjective "new" (22; compare 65:17–18)—this framing phrase thus signals both compositional continuity and thematic inversion. "From Creation to New Creation" is the theme not only of Isa 1—66, but also of the comprehensive literary work of which it is a part: "A Book of Remembrance." As elsewhere in the book, the circle of world-embracing Judaism (19–20) finds its center in the holy city (18, 22–24), thus portraying the theme which may serve as the key for a description of the theology of the Book of Isaiah.

A sermon may explore the manner in which "the ends of the earth" (49:6) is illustrated by the names of peoples which appear rarely in the Bible and refer to their distant places of residence (compare 19 with 2:16 [Tarshish] and Jer 46:9 [Lud]). The dispersed descendants of the patriarchs living among those nations are evidently still ignorant of the arguments presented in Isaiah (and in "The Law and the Prophets" generally), to the effect that the Lord God of Israel is the only one God, supreme in power and worshiped only in Jerusalem with offerings and sacrifices. In other words, the manifestations of their piety are not (no longer/not yet) in accord with those stipulated in the Law of Moses; they are thus to a certain extent comparable to the post-exilic (contemporary) military Jewish colonists on the island of Elephantine in Upper Egypt, who adhered to a variant form of devotion to the God of Israel.

Finally, preachers may deal with the way in which the book's concluding lines emphasize the rhythm of the observation of holy seasons, notably that of new moon and sabbath (22–23). Do they not mark periods of rest and renewal in the flow of time and thus become symbols of the people's identity and religious loyalty? The Law of Moses, with reference to either the Exodus from Egypt or the Lord's creation of the terrestrial realm in six days, repeatedly calls the faithful to such observance (Exod 20:8–11; 31:12–17; Deut 5:12–15). Does not Jewish custom still today welcome each sabbath as one welcomes a bride? And does the Isaianic passage not also provide the setting for the affirmation of an early Christian writing that there still remains for the people of God "a sabbath rest" (Heb 4:9 [3:1—4:13])?

Bibliography

Clements, R. E., *Isaiah 1—39* (London/Grand Rapids: Marshall, Morgan & Scott/Wm. B. Eerdmans, 1980).

———, *Isaiah and the Deliverance of Jerusalem: A Study of the Interpretation of Prophecy in the Old Testament* (Sheffield: JSOT Press, 1980).

Herbert, A. S., *The Book of the Prophet Isaiah, 1-39* (Cambridge/New York: Cambridge University Press, 1973).

Heschel, A. J., *The Prophets* (New York: Harper & Row, 1962).

Holladay, W. L., *Isaiah: Scroll of a Prophetic Heritage* (Grand Rapids: Wm. B. Eerdmans, 1978).

Jensen, J., *Isaiah 1—39* (Wilmington/Dublin: Michael Glazier/Gill & Macmillan, 1984).

Kaiser, O., *Isaiah 1—12* (2d ed.) and *Isaiah 13—39* (London/Philadelphia: SCM Press/Westminster Press, 1983, 1974).

McKenzie, J. L. *Second Isaiah* (Garden City: Doubleday, 1974).

Rad, G. von, *The Message of the Prophets* (London/New York: SCM Press/Harper & Row, 1968).

Schmitt, J. J., *Isaiah and His Interpreters* (New York/Mahwah: Paulist Press, 1986).

Scullion, J., *Isaiah 40—66* (Wilmington/Dublin: Michael Glazier/Gill & Macmillan, 1982).

Westermann, C., *Isaiah 40—66* (London/Philadelphia:SCM Press/Westminster Press, 1969).

Whybray, R. N., *Isaiah 40—66* (London/Grand Rapids: Marshall, Morgan & Scott/Wm. B. Eerdmans, 1981).